SO-BFA-947

Praise for Essays from *Becoming 65,* a monthly feature column in the *Bucks County Herald.*

* Delightful, well-chosen words...well-observed and picturesque. I simply was captured and forced to read on... Hans H.
* Well-done article. Thanks for sharing such a personal and compelling story! Liz G.
* Loved your cheapskate column. Our mothers should have written a book on the uses for used foil! Carolyn H.
* We are better men as a result of [your writings]. Chris W. and Frank L.
* You are such a good writer—I felt I was there. What a beautiful experience. Mary M.
* I read your essay and found it very moving...I truly do believe that we all do the best we can in any given moment. Kate A.
* Your article jumped off the page at me this morning! I've been procrastinating in sending holiday cards because I didn't know what to say. I'm writing to share that it became clear as I read your [piece]... My husband agreed it would be a [message] he'd like to share too. Judy L.
* My [wife] and I got a little teary reading your article—we were very touched and moved by the whole [piece]. Gerry H.
* Keep writing these breezy, whimsical pieces and...you will be summoned by the staff of the *Boston Globe* or the *New York Times.* Christopher W.
* Your article is now front and center on my fridge. I look forward to your writings. Wendy D.
* You certainly can tell a story. Thank you for the beautiful way you told mine. I am so grateful! Cristina S.

- Your current column is not only beautifully written but resonated with me. CKW
- When I read your article, *"Driving 'Miss Crazy,'"* this week, it reminded me of a travel article my 11-year-old daughter and I wrote in 1982. Ray G.
- As always, I enjoy your writing and appreciate your friendship. One day at a time, may we both be able to give, receive and enjoy the many blessings [being in] our 70s bring to us. Loretta W.
- I just wanted to thank you for the beautiful article regarding our mutual friend...He was loved by everyone in our office and will be greatly missed. I'll share your article with our staff. Michael H.
- We enjoy reading your column, but this one was really special for us...Thanks for all the enjoyment and inspiration your columns provide for us and I'm certain for many others in the community. Your column contributes greatly. Keep it up! Bill and Mary Lee L.
- Loved your article. Life is never dull that is for sure. Yvonne L.
- I am catching up on missed newspapers and saw your sensitive article—thank you for sharing [this] story so beautifully. Susan W.

Also by Kay G. Rock

Everything I Know About Relationships
I Learned Dancing
A Kindle eBook   Available at www.amazon.com

Over the Hill and Gaining Speed

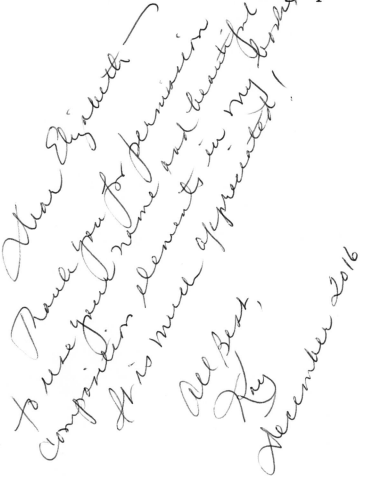

Dear Elizabeth —

Thank you for permission
to use your name and beautiful
composition elements in my book.
It is much appreciated!

All Best,
Kay

December 2016

Over the Hill and Gaining Speed

REFLECTIONS IN RETIREMENT

Kay G. Rock

OVER THE HILL AND GAINING SPEED: Reflections in Retirement.
Copyright © 2016 Kay G. Rock. All rights reserved. No part of this publication may be reproduced, distributed, or transmitted in any form or by any means, including photocopying, recording or other electronic or mechanical methods, without the prior written permission of the author. Exceptions would be in the case of brief quotations embodied in critical reviews and certain other noncommercial uses permitted by copyright law and which credit the author. For permission or requests, contact www.createspace.com.
Printed in the United States of America.

www.CreateSpace.com

Photographs are courtesy of the author unless otherwise captioned or credited.

Rock, Kay G.
    Over the Hill and Gaining Speed: Reflections in Retirement. Kay G. Rock, edited by Alice Lawler—1st Edition.
A collection of Kay G. Rock's monthly columns from the *Bucks County Herald*, 2011-2015, Lahaska, Pennsylvania.
ISBN-13: 9781537594002
ISBN-10: 1537594001

1. Life Cycles and Transitions—Observations in Retirement
2. Daily Life and Relationships
3. Travel
4. Inspiration

For SLR, with love
Thank you for the space and the Space

Table of Contents

Author's Notes

A TIME FOR PARTING (OR, HOW THIS BOOK CAME TO BE)

IN MY JANUARY 2015 COLUMN for the *Bucks County Herald*, I noted that I would celebrate my 70th birthday that year. I once again banged the drum for discernment when attaining a seminal event (but really anytime), and have followed my own recommendation with a year-long "...review of where I've been, where I am now, and where I want to go with however many years I have remaining."

I was bold in that column. I made an announcement. As the self-acknowledged key stakeholder in my life, I indicated I had begun the work of compiling my articles into a book. I then crawled farther out on the limb—arching it dangerously close to the ground—and said I hoped to have said book published and on the market before the end of the year. SNAP. It didn't happen.

It didn't happen for wonderful reasons: travels to Key West and Colorado, the birth of a new grandson in Santa Fe, family weddings, family anniversaries, a 70th birthday celebration, a long-awaited retreat in Hawaii, a gorgeous extended autumn, and the enlivening company of grandchildren.

So why, you might ask, at my age and with the fullness of life, do I want to hassle myself with producing a book? I don't know. In fact, the very notion is daunting. During my year of reflection,

I have come to terms with the reality that there are certain things in this life I won't ever achieve. I will never be a ballet dancer. There are lands I will never see. Books I will never read. Literal and figurative mountains I will never climb. So be it. I've been as fortunate as any in what I have experienced, and am now ready to start accepting life's growing limitations. Sort of. Maybe. Well, mostly. Actually only a little bit.

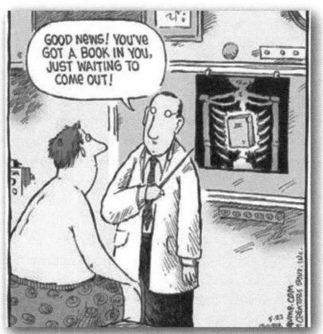

Cartoon used with permission of David Coverly and speedbump.com

I want to write a book. This is a desire that will not go away. Like a caged thing, it paces and prowls within me, restless to the core. I wish it would just go to a corner and lie down. But it doesn't. I consider the challenge of rewrites, permissions, self-publishing, marketing. Ugh. And yet it won't go away. It is a vision that kicks and punches, needing to be born. And so my undisciplined, easily distracted self must start to clear my plate and thereby, hopefully, gain some focus. For this reason, this will be my final column.

December 2015 marks five years of writing for the *Bucks County Herald*. It has been a wonderful ride and I have enjoyed it immensely. But as Ecclesiastes reminds us:

> *"For everything there is a season,*
> *and a time for every matter under heaven...*
> *A time for remembering, a time for parting.**

The Bucks County Herald, December 17, 2015

**And a time for writing the damn book!*

Part One:
On the Road

"Travel.

As much as you can.

As far as you can.

As long as you can.

Life's not meant to be lived in one place."

ANONYMOUS

The Next Phase of the Journey

My mother was at the supermarket when she was stopped in her tracks by an announcement over the loudspeaker—Japan had surrendered and World War II was finally over. It was August 1945 and she was eight months pregnant with me. I was born a month later, making me now 65 years of age.

Sixty-five. Yikes! When I was growing up it sounded like "The End." It was the age when retirement began (should you have lived so long) and everything else stopped—with a thud. Or so my younger self believed. It's amazing how young 65 now feels. Now that I've chronologically turned 65, a Confucian perspective of *becoming* 65 seems more appropriate. Sixty-five is more than an age. It is a transition process and we must grow into it. On some level, of course, I had a birthday and TURNED 65, as one calendar page followed the next. But have I yet *become* 65? And what might that mean?

In *Wind, Sand and Stars*, philosopher and pilot Antoine de Saint-Exupéry reflects on the Spanish Civil War and tells of a bookkeeper who has put down his green eyeshade and answered the call to fight for his passion and belief. At this crucial juncture, Saint-Exupéry rhetorically asks: "Sergeant, Sergeant, what will you do with this gift of life?"

As I become 65, I ask myself the same question: what will I do with this gift of life? The ambiguity surrounding the duration of the journey heightens my sense of urgency and need for discernment. Except I'm also really tired and the thought of urgency of any kind makes me want to take a nap.

There are not only the philosophical questions to consider but also the practical: When and how do I apply for Social Security? Which Medicare plan should I take? Will I ever stand on my head again or become airborne during a Lindy Hop? But I digress. The real question is, "What will I do with this gift of life?"

I know I'm beyond the final half of life, but where am I? Final third? Final quarter? Final…oh let's not go down this path. We will never know for sure when this fragile gift will end—only that someday it will. It's a scary thought. I don't want it to end. Especially now when I feel so much life potential may be awaiting me. I'm filled with contradictory thoughts and feelings.

Recently I attended a professional development seminar featuring David Ulrich, a renowned professor of business at the University of Michigan. I became familiar with him through case studies while in graduate school. I was thrilled to actually meet Ulrich in person. Ulrich identified five key areas he addresses when coaching a senior executive. I no longer qualify for the executive part, but I'm definitely senior, so I paid close attention. He emphasized that WE are the key stakeholders in our lives and as such we need to continually address: the Physical, the Emotional, the Social, the Intellectual, and the Spiritual aspects of these lives.

I may not be able to do all this and work too. Maybe I should retire? After all I am 65—the speed limit for open highways. The age when life begins (you have heard that 65 is the new 40, right?). Time to put the pedal to the metal—for if not now, then when? Fasten your seat belts. We're going for a ride!

The Bucks County Herald, January 20, 2011

A Capitol Day

WITH OUR HEADS TIPPED BACK and our open mouths comically mirroring the giant concave above us, we stared in awe at the majestic dome of our State Capitol. Intentionally designed by Philadelphian Joseph Huston to be "A Palace of Art," Pennsylvania's Capitol complex is a priceless architectural and artistic treasure which has been deemed a National Historic Landmark. But first and foremost, this State Capitol is a public building belonging to the citizens of Pennsylvania.

Our reason for being here started at a silent auction fundraiser. The state senator representing my local district donated a "Day in the Capital," comprised of a variety of events including an introduction in the Senate Chamber. My friend's eyes locked with mine. There was no question of anyone else winning this bid. It was OURS.

Our day started at the Governor's Mansion, a beautiful home fronting the mighty Susquehanna River. Gracious as well as grand, each room seemed to open itself to us in welcome. It was easy to appreciate how such a residence could embrace and hold the many necessary business and social gatherings of a governor, as well as be a home. The lush and meticulous landscaping was highlighted by the spectacular Jane Shafer (former First Lady of Pennsylvania) Rose Garden.

After entering the Capitol, we had a brief visit to the Senate offices and the Governor's Reception Room. Here we first saw the site and sight of several Violet Oakley murals. Lunch was provided and then we were whisked off to the take-your-breath-away green marble and gold-accented Senate Chamber, resplendent with additional massive murals by Violet Oakley, depicting key events in Pennsylvania's history. Our state senators met us there for photos and graciously spent a few minutes of precious time (fiscal year-end was only three weeks away), talking with us about our concerns and theirs. We then went to the gallery area and were introduced to the Senate.

Pennsylvania's Capitol is not only distinguished by an unmatched collection of paintings, murals, stained glass, furnishings, and locally-crafted Mercer tiles—all of which represent some aspect of Pennsylvania's achievements in labor, industry, art, and history—it is also the working site of all three branches of state government. It is a living, vital entity brimming with daily activity in the midst of museum-worthy surroundings. The day we visited, hundreds of trade union representatives were holding a rally in the Capitol Rotunda. Like a mountain's echo, their speeches and rousing responses reverberated up the three-tiered gallery into the 272-foot dome, which was inspired by Michelangelo's design for St. Peter's Basilica in Rome. Their numbers packed the Mercer tile-embellished floor and filled the sweeping Grand Staircase, deliberately modeled after the Paris Opera House.

After the senators were summoned to their caucuses, we were given a tour of the House Chamber and the Pennsylvania Supreme Court. The House Chamber murals are by Edwin Austin Abbey. Upon Abbey's premature death in 1911—and based on the excellence of Oakley's work in the Governor's Reception Room—the remaining murals for the Senate Chamber and Supreme Court were commissioned to Violet Oakley. She was the first American female artist to receive a commission for murals for a public building. Ironically, however, she never entered the legislative chambers. Women were not allowed.

The dedication of this awe-inspiring Capitol building was held in 1906 and attended by then-President Theodore Roosevelt. He declared it to be "… the handsomest building I ever saw." It is the geographic, legislative and artistic center of the Commonwealth, and our visit there was truly "a capital Capitol experience!"

The Bucks County Herald, July 18, 2013

Photo used with permission of the Pennsylvania State Archives MG-152.4 S. Emerson Bolton Collection, Photographs, Dedication of New Capitol Building, October 4, 1906 Image: President Theodore Roosevelt "President opening his address."

R&R Retreat

"WHEN I RETIRE," I PROMISED myself, "I will give myself an R&R retreat." I even had the spot in mind—a yoga center in western Massachusetts that I had always found intriguing. Weeks and months passed, and finally I did retire. The self-promised getaway idea twisted and turned in the universe, like a leaf trying to break free from its branch. This twisting in the wind of a pre-retirement plum went on for additional weeks, months, and even years when, quite unbidden (perhaps through universal consciousness?), I received a catalog in the mail. The cover was emblazoned with just the right words: Winter Sale for R&R retreats. If a guest stayed three nights, two nights were free. All activities and room and board were included. My moment had come.

In January I set out solo, just me and the road. I had not driven to the Berkshires alone before and somehow missed a well-marked exit for the Taconic Parkway. Frustrated and a little bit lost, I took the next exit and was advised to continue on to Connecticut and follow Route 7N straight into my destination. This unplanned detour, although longer, was an amazing serendipity that led me through a dazzling iconic New England fairyland. The route followed the Housatonic River snaking from one side of the road to the other, its frozen edges ruffled by lively white water. It wended through snow-covered state forest lands, and passed through charming villages and covered bridges. It was truly breathtaking. Sometimes getting lost is a gift.

Finally arriving only slightly after dark, I checked in, unpacked, and hustled to dinner before the dining hall closed. I don't know what I expected really, but the large, noisy, very institutional dining hall with finite service hours surprised me. Fundamentally, the facility is a school. It offers certifications for different levels of yoga instruction and massage therapy, as well as continuing education credits for nurses, psychologists, physical therapists, and more. As I entered the dining hall, I was greeted by two long buffet lines—one for vegetarians and the other also for vegetarians—except for the occasional tray of fish. Initially, the buffet struck me as little more than a cornucopia of bird seed. However, after a meal or two, I came to enjoy sampling a wide variety of well-prepared wholesome foods, with or without meat. The soups were delicious and the breads toothsomely gorgeous. If I had someone to prepare such food for me regularly, I could be about 80 percent vegetarian. Why only 80 percent? Honestly, I just enjoy meat too much. One night, the food service staff pandered to us carnivores with pans filled to the brim with roasted chicken, mashed potatoes and gravy. It felt like Thanksgiving.

The four-story building was a hive of activity with people buzzing to events, attending classes, and hanging out in the café, solarium, or lounges. Formerly a Jesuit seminary, the facility is long on function and short on aesthetics. However, my private room was clean and contained all the necessities, and public spaces were pleasant. For those of us in the R&R program, a daily list of activities was provided. The first day, I wanted to try almost everything. It took only one session to realize that overbooking oneself is a contradiction at an R&R retreat.

I quickly got sensible and limited myself to one yoga class daily, plus an additional movement activity such as a noon-time dance class, tai chi (so beautiful), or a guided hike in the mountains. (Although the facility is institutional, the grounds, nestled in the Berkshire Mountains, are beautiful and provide many wonderful hiking opportunities.)

In the evenings I tried guided meditation, chanting and drumming. I even took the plunge (pun intended) with a sauna, hot tub, and ice pool combo—which supposedly boosts the immune system. Of course, it only works if one survives.

An extra treat (for an extra fee) was a wonderful massage. In between activities, I never missed a meal, and still found plenty of time to read, explore the buildings and grounds, and doze off in a lounge chair in the warmth of the sunny solarium.

My trip home was confident and uneventful, with not even one missed exit or anxious moment. People ask me what the retreat was like. I smile beatifically, placing my palms together in the center of my chest and intone, " Shanthi, shanthi, shanthi: peace, peace, peace."

The Bucks County Herald, March 20, 2013

Of Baseball and Battlefields

PART I: BASEBALL

AH, SPRING! THE FEEL OF sun on one's face, the smell of the earth, bulbs and buds popping all around. But for baseball fans, spring doesn't really arrive until they hear the call to "Play Ball!" To push the season, my husband and I decided to go to Cooperstown, New York, and the National Baseball Hall of Fame and Museum. It was March and freezing cold, but baseball was in the air everywhere. Abner Doubleday, often cited as the "inventor" of baseball, lived in Cooperstown during his school years. His role in baseball history has since been disavowed, but Doubleday Field in the center of town still proudly carries his name.

The museum hosts baseball memorabilia both old and new. It is an awesome space to explore and a wonderfully nostalgic excuse to travel to a quaint upstate New York town. The experience starts with a film—in a theater designed as a baseball stadium—followed by a self-guided tour of intuitively flowing exhibit spaces. As we meandered through the unfolding of baseball history, I began to understand that baseball is not just a game—it is an intrinsic part of our history as a nation, incorporating themes of immigration, integration, and even war. (Many players served in the military and, during World War II, Roosevelt thought it important that the games continue, to bolster national morale.)

The Baseball Museum is filled with more memories than grandma's attic. In one display, I encountered the iconic Yankee team of the 1950s, and was immediately transported to my childhood living room where my father and I cheered every run and bemoaned every out, from one World Series to the next. We laughed at Casey Stengel's grumpy demeanor and duck-like extension of his neck and head. Wham! Like a well-struck ball, I suddenly realized baseball was part of my personal history too.

"Hey, I remember that!" I exclaimed to no one in particular, on seeing the jersey Doc Halladay wore when he pitched his perfect game. My husband and I laughed in glee spotting Wilson Valdez's cap, remembering the May 2011 game when Valdez became only the second ballplayer (the other was Babe Ruth in 1921) to start the game in the field and end it as the winning pitcher—during the Phillies' incredible 19-inning marathon against the Cincinnati Reds. Ah, good times.

The Baseball Hall of Fame is really two museums in one: a museum of the history of baseball (and the American experience), and a separate Hall of Fame lined with brass bas-reliefs of key people in the sport. The plaques are beautiful art as well as history, and the serene Hall exudes an aura of sacred space. All conversations, as if on cue, became subdued and whispery as people entered. Plaques commemorate owners, managers, and others who have served. One is for a black woman, Effa Manley, a Philadelphia-born co-owner and business manager of the Newark Eagles of the Negro League. She was a trailblazing owner and tireless crusader for civil rights. She made her team a social force off the field and a baseball force on it, and the fans loved her for it.

Jackie Robinson, the first black man to play Major League ball, is acknowledged for not only his baseball achievements, but also for his pivotal role in the future course of the game and American history. "Displayed tremendous courage and poise in 1947 when he integrated the modern Major Leagues in the face of intense adversity," reads his plaque. Across the Hall, Pee Wee Reese, a white player from Kentucky, is similarly honored and acknowledged for being "Instrumental in easing acceptance of Jackie Robinson as baseball's first black performer."

Photo Credit: National Baseball Hall of Fame Library
Cooperstown, New York
Jackie Robinson and Harold Henry "Pee Wee" Reese

These plaques serve as a reminder that we all need courage to create a more just society. These institutions demonstrate that baseball is more than a diversion and its greatest heroes did more than just play the game. They were catalysts who changed our lives and wove themselves into the diverse tapestry that is American culture and history.

Ball fields and battlefields may not seem to have much in common, but a key figure links them both.

⟨⸺⟩

PART II: BATTLEFIELDS

In his recent book, *The Joy of Old Age*, author Oliver Sacks notes that as one has an ever longer experience of life, "[one gains]...a vivid, lived sense of history not possible at an earlier age." Perhaps that explains my ever increasing penchant to visit museums and historic sites and meander my way through all sorts of memorabilia. I have always enjoyed history, but today museums offer insights that didn't manifest for my younger self. Museums and significant sites help concentrate my understanding of the big picture, and focus my attention on the humanity of individual stories and legacies.

Part I of this article explores American history through the lens of baseball. More than just a game, it was also a symbolic battlefield of social justice and integration. Soon after visiting Cooperstown, we traveled to central Pennsylvania and explored an actual battleground. The famous Battle of Gettysburg was the largest battle of our Civil War and the largest battle ever fought in North America. The Union Army of the Potomac numbered approximately 85,000 men while the Confederacy's Army of Northern Virginia commanded 75,000. At the end of three days of fighting (July 1–3, 1863), total casualties exceeded 23,000—a horrific loss of life and limb sustained by both sides. As the armies retreated, the people of Gettysburg were left to deal with the carnage, and to try and understand what had happened and what their lives had now become.

Our pilgrimage—and indeed it felt as if it were just that—started in the new Visitors Center and Museum. Impressive scholarship, curation, and multimedia offerings provided a macro perspective that brought forth the grand scale and historic sweep of all that transpired on those fateful days over 150 years ago. It gave us pause to think of the high passions on both sides that led to such a battle and such a war. The human cost sobered us as did the historic impact. Although the war would continue for another two years, Gettysburg is generally considered a key turning point for the North which led to the ultimate preservation of the Union and the abolition of the institution of slavery.

On day two, we hired a private guide to drive us to key sites and explain their significance. As we moved from place to place, he masterfully recreated what transpired there. Even without actual re-enactors, we could envision the ferocity of these engagements. I was unprepared for the vastness of the landscape and the dispersion of conflicts strung out over miles in every direction. The logistics of moving men and animals, artillery and ammunition, food and supplies boggled my mind.

We learned of communication challenges and miscues and how they often became a determining factor in success or failure. We marveled at how unimpressive Little Round Top appeared from below—and how imposing from above. Day two provided us with a field-level view of the miscues, operational challenges, and intensity of battle faced by both sides.

Gettysburg has over a thousand markers and monuments. There were several we wished to see on our last day. The misty rain and low clouds evoked the cannon smoke of battle. In this eerie fog, as we read names listed on markers, long-ago emotions became palpable, rising as ghosts from the once blood-soaked fields: fear, frenzy, fury, hope, despair, disappointment, determination, exaltation, defeat, pressure, apprehension, relief, confusion, camaraderie, isolation, agony, and anger—a panoply of human feelings swirled around us in the haze.

Statues came alive. We felt Buford's anxiety as he surveyed the oncoming Confederate forces, Lee's agony as he watched the devastation of Pickett's charge, and Meade's mental gear-shifting on being named commander of the Union's largest army only three days before the battle ensued. Meade was a military engineer who only wanted to design and build lighthouses. Barnegat Lighthouse in New Jersey is one of Meade's designs.

**Major General
Abner Doubleday**

We spot Abner Doubleday's statue—the same Abner Doubleday of Cooperstown fame. His commander, John Reynolds, provided the reinforcements Buford so anxiously awaited, but was killed 20 minutes into battle. Doubleday was called up to lead the corps. Although badly outnumbered, he and his soldiers acquitted themselves honorably and fought ferociously—until the corps to his right collapsed and forced retreat. Unfortunately that commander filed a false report to Meade, absolving himself and blaming Doubleday for the defeat. Meade subsequently replaced Doubleday, a career US Army officer, with a more junior officer, creating a lasting enmity between the two men.

We position ourselves in front of the monument and look up. Doubleday stands tall on his marble base, gazing into the woods where he and his men fought with such tenacity. And yet, one senses his disappointment and rage. Unlike Meade, Doubleday longed to be a military leader, but chicanery denied him his due.

In an ironic twist of historic proportions, we remember Meade as a military man rather than a designer of famous lighthouses.

And we remember Doubleday not for "gallant and meritorious [military] service," but for a baseball field in upstate New York, honoring him for a game he never invented.

The Bucks County Herald, May 15, 2014

Cross-Country Impressions

THIS SUMMER, MY ABOVE-AVERAGE HUSBAND, our handsome dog, and I once again set off cross-country, covering some 2,600-plus miles over a period of nine days. Like last year, we incorporated several tourist stops, as well as visits with friends and family. A cross-country venture is not only a great way to reconnect—it is also a first-hand, up-close-and-personal opportunity to experience the varied sights and textures of this great land of ours. We careered through farmlands and fields, mountains and valleys, forests and deserts. We drank in big skies and endless horizons. Some of our observations were inspiring; some were painful. We observed not only the beauty of nature but also her brutality as we witnessed the aftermath of the violent *derechos*—straight-line storms with hurricane force—that wreaked havoc on several Mid-Atlantic states and left several hundred thousand people without electricity and water for weeks. As we angled west-southwest, we observed the slow immolation of once green hills into dusty brown flats and wished for pipelines that could transport water from flooded areas to these parched and burning lands.

We took to the Interstate Highway System—the Eisenhower Interstate—and observed the marvelous mobility of these United States. On our first day out, our license plate game garnered 33 different US states as well as three Canadian provinces and Guam. Spotting an Alaska tag on day one was a high-five moment.

Americans are on the move—visiting and vacationing, meeting and greeting, learning and sharing, working and playing, celebrating and mourning. We saw legions of semis—most pulling two trailers at a time. They motored on, one right after the other, alternative "trains" unrestricted by rails. They were hauling everything from carpets to cabbages, horses to housewares, lumber to La-Z-Boys, milk to metals, packages to poultry, timber to toys. They hauled eastbound and westbound—crossing from state to state without stopping for customs, changing language, or converting currency. In Tennessee we noticed an armada of utility vehicles, like a parade of grasshoppers—heading east on I-81 into Virginia and beyond, to help restore power to storm-ravaged areas in neighboring states. Americans were on the move to aid other Americans in need. The impressions were indelible.

All this social and economic mobility is greatly enabled by our Interstate Highway System. An interregional highway system was first recommended by Franklin D. Roosevelt in a 1939 address to Congress. Political opponents considered it "more New Deal jitterbug economics." The idea languished until Dwight D. Eisenhower advocated for it in his 1954 State of the Union address. Two key events made Eisenhower a strong proponent of a federal highway system. The first occurred during a post-World War I impediment-filled transcontinental military trip across the United States in 1919. The second was his first-hand experience of the advantages of Germany's autobahn system during and after World War II.

According to CNN correspondent Tamar Jacoby, Eisenhower's highway proposal was "...the health-care legislation of its day—an epic battle." Competing political interests and powerful lobbies blocked progress for nearly two years. Then, in a stunning reversal, everyone suddenly seemed to realize that the benefits would more than outweigh the costs. Congress became more interested in strategic problem-solving than ideological purity, and the bill was passed. On June 29, 1956, the Federal Aid Highway Act was presented to

Eisenhower—in a hospital bed at Walter Reed Hospital where he was confined due to a recent heart attack. There, he signed into law the vision he had so long championed, without fanfare or ceremony. At an initial cost of $50 billion, it comprised more than two-thirds of the federal budget in 1956, and is often referred to as "the biggest public works program since the Pyramids."

In his 1963 memoir, *Mandate for Change*, Eisenhower defined this Act as his most important domestic achievement. He stated that more than any other single action by government since the end of World War II, this law would change the face of America in ways that were beyond calculation. Many historians agree. The Interstate Highway System is part of the American culture and way of life. It is a major contributor to job creation, daily transportation, interstate commerce, local, regional, and international connectivity, tourism, humanitarian aid and evacuation, and—if needed—defense. Long stretches of the Interstates are straight as a runway—in case they ever need to be used for military aircraft.

Directly or indirectly, every US citizen benefits, one way or another. Infrastructure matters. Funding for this system is not a given and continually requires Congressional approval. We urge Congress, as they did in 1956, to once again put aside differences and consider the common good and make this a permanently funded budget item. Such vision and cooperation would continue to provide domestic and global benefits.*

The Bucks County Herald, August 16, 2012

The "Fixing America's Surface Transportation Act" ("FAST Act") was passed by Congress and signed into law by President Obama on December 4, 2015, once again providing long-term funding support for critical transportation projects, including federal highways.

Land of Enchantment

AT FIRST THERE WAS SILENCE; then, a hissing sound. Then, the roar of fire as waves of heat and expanding air rolled out around us. Huge fans bellowed, towers of flame rose up, and slumbering giants gradually stirred and awoke all around us. They pulled mightily against their tethers and fought the strength and force of their handlers, dichotomous forces battling against conflicting desires. They wanted to be free, to fly and shoot tongues of fire. They wanted to float over the Land of Enchantment, and lure all who saw them to succumb to their spell.

This dragons' lair is actually a huge field in central New Mexico, home of the Albuquerque International Balloon Festival, the world's premiere ballooning event. This year, 600 balloons were registered, from all over the globe. As we walked amongst the sounds and struggles, surrounded by light-as-air behemoths, we felt magic as we watched the metamorphoses of these gorgeous inflatables being readied for a special evening event known as "Balloon Glow." As the balloons expanded, we saw many in the traditional Brussels sprout-shape, festooned in beautiful patterns, colors, and flags. Others were fanciful special shapes that included a scuba diver, a trio of bees, a white cow, a pink pig, an astronaut, and a huge Wells Fargo stagecoach.

Our night was crystal clear. Venus was shining brilliantly as the darkening sky gradually filled with stars. The barest sliver of a moon rose over the 5,000-foot-high desert horizon, dangling like a precious pendant. I couldn't decide if the heavens were the perfect backdrop for the balloons, or if the balloons were the perfect foreground for the sky. Of course, it didn't matter. New Mexico is the Land of Enchantment—a place made to enjoy the magic.

As the balloons won their identities and the crews subdued their desire to take flight, the master of ceremonies began the countdown over the loudspeakers. Soon the eager crowd joined in, like a premature New Year's Eve celebration, shouting "10-9-8-7-6-5-4-3-2-1: ALL BURN!" The dark outlines of shifting shapes suddenly transformed into a riot of color, noise, and novelty, as the pilots simultaneously engaged their burners and filled the translucent forms with light and magic, over and over and over again. We were enchanted.

When I was 11 years old, I saw David Niven play Phileas Fogg in the star-studded film, *Around the World in 80 Days*. I have been fascinated by hot air balloons ever since, and attending this fiesta is the fulfillment of a bucket-list dream. In addition to the "Glow," we also attended a sunrise Mass Ascension, with hundreds of balloons from many nations lifting off in orchestrated waves. They filled the dark, chill morning air like bubbles from some Brobdingnagian soap machine.

As the sun rose over the craggy crest of the Sandia Mountains to the east, its rays pierced directly through the ropes of an elegant balloon emblazoned with the legend, "Defy Gravity." It was a mystical moment. Was it a reminder not to let things weigh us down? Or perhaps a prod to find our fire and rise up? As more and more balloons filled the sky, I decided maybe they weren't bubbles after all, but rather ascending prayers. New Mexico is the Land of Enchantment. This Balloon Festival is just one of its magical spells. I am in its thrall.

The Bucks County Herald, October 17, 2013

Driving "Miss Crazy"

THIS SUMMER WE TRAVELED TO Scotland with four friends. We saw wonderful sights: Edinburgh Castle, the Highlands and Isle of Skye, and Glasgow's soaring Central Station. We heard glorious sounds: the Military Tattoo featuring hundreds of bagpipers *en masse*, the distinctive Highland dialect, an actor reciting Robert Burns' poetry (in Scots) from a parapet at Stirling Castle. We experienced delicious tastes: Scottish salmon, cranachan, fish and chips, and wee drams of single malt.

At the end of our tour, each couple went their separate way on self-guided adventures. My husband and I rented a car to continue our journey down through England. This was a brave thing to do—drive a rental car through England, that is. Britons, as you know, drive on the wrong side of the road.

My husband did an awesome job getting us around, but despite his capable chauffeuring, I was still experiencing major crises of perception. My mind revolted at the mirror image experience posed by driving in Britain. I sincerely believe if someone had held a gun to my head and said, "Drive here, or else!" I would have said, "Shoot me!"

I rode in the passenger seat, which, of course, felt like the driver's seat—and which soon led to my transformation from a relaxed traveler into "Miss Crazy." If the car wandered too close to the curb, I gripped the arm rest and yelled, "Close, close, CLOSE!" On narrow country roads, (where signs actually said "On-coming cars may be in the middle of the road"), "Miss Crazy" yelled—with every oncoming car—"Car, car, CAR!" Right turns were a seat-gripping, eye-widening event. Roundabouts—of which there were more in a 30-mile stretch in England than in the entire state of New Jersey—put me into a full imitation of Edvard Munch's "The Scream."

As the navigator, I found myself trying to decipher signs crowded with circles, arrows, and hilariously cumbersome names like "The Wallops-near-Bramble-side," "Sudbury-on-the-Lea-over-Water," or "Flow-Gently-Sweet-Afton." One needed an Evelyn Wood speed reading certificate to determine which arrow to follow to which destination and just where one should exit the roundabout to get there! "Miss Crazy" had no choice but to yell, "Circle, circle, CIRCLE," to allow time to determine if we were to exit at "eleven o'clock," "one o'clock," or "three o'clock." Sometimes it took so long we got dizzy. Fortunately, once in the roundabout, we had right-of-way. Equally auspicious, my husband remained calm in the midst of my panic attacks.

Driving challenges aside, our travels through the Lake District, Midlands, and ultimately the Cotswolds, provided glorious scenery and experiences, a highlight of which was a tour of Highclere Castle, filming location of the popular PBS series, *Downton Abbey*. I thoroughly enjoyed descending the staircase, pretending to be Lady Mary; sitting in the library imagining having tea with the Dowager Countess; and relaxing on the beautiful grounds of "Downton," fantasizing we were "Lord and Lady Rock."

"Lord and Lady Rock"

These diversions enabled me to once again relax and accept the fantasy and fun, as well as the beauty and history—and yes, driving rules—of Britain. Or perhaps I was beginning to adapt. Whatever the reason, "Miss Crazy" no longer accompanied us on our travels—she had been given "the boot"!

The Bucks County Herald, October 16, 2014

Bearing Witness

LAST MONTH WE EXPERIENCED A historic occasion. Pope Francis, the Bishop of Rome, made his first visit to the United States. He visited Washington, DC, New York City, and Philadelphia. All of his stops were significant, but I was particularly touched by his visit to bear witness at the 9/11 Memorial in lower Manhattan. Less than a week before, my husband and I were visiting New York and also made an intentional pilgrimage to Ground Zero. It was a powerful experience.

We stood at the edge of one of the memorial reflecting pools and lightly traced our fingers across an engraved name, outlining each letter. Each of the nearly 3,000 victims from 1993 and 2001 was remembered by an inscription. One of my tracings was of a woman and her unborn child. Others were fathers, mothers, spouses, sons, daughters, aunts, uncles, nieces, nephews, cousins, neighbors, friends and colleagues.

**9/11 Memorial,
New York City**

Each name meant something to someone and everything to others. And all of them mean something to every American. We feel their loss in our hearts, minds, and fingertips. *"No day shall erase you from the memory of time."*

This summer, on a road trip across the US, we visited many fun and indulgent places. In the midst of our easy-going rambles, we deliberately included a visit to the Oklahoma City National Memorial and Museum in Oklahoma City, Oklahoma, to remember those victims and their families. *"It was a day like any other"*—until suddenly and violently, it wasn't. The main impact of the blast hit the on site day care center filled with children. Innocents.

At the museum next to the memorial, we heard the start of a recorded meeting, business as usual. Then: the roar of the blast, followed by the screams. It was visceral. It made me angry. It made me cry. But mostly, it made me want to touch each one of the "chairs" on the memorial grounds and say: "You mattered. You will not be forgotten."

Photo credit: Oklahoma City National Memorial and Museum Image: "Field of Empty Chairs (@Night)"

And just as we remember those who were lost, it is imperative to recognize the challenges of those who survived—not only those who were in the buildings that day, but all the family and friends of those who went to work one morning and never returned, all the parents who would never again hug and kiss their little toddlers. The pain—on all counts—has made an imprint on our collective psyche. "*We Come Here to Remember.*"

Later this year we will travel to Hawaii.* We will lounge on Waikiki Beach, snorkel, drink pastel concoctions adorned with pineapple chunks and umbrellas, and marvel at fantastic coastlines and waterfalls. But first—first, we will visit Pearl Harbor. To bear witness. To pay our respects. To honor all those whose lives were lost on that fateful day. We will learn about the USS Arizona and the USS Missouri—evocative remnants of "*the day that will live in infamy.*"

All these memorials are dignified testimonies to our resilience as individuals and as a nation. They offer comfort, strength and hope, even as they underscore the impact, waste, and ripple effect of violence. And so we make these trips and stand watch—at least for a time—over those who were in our collective lives, to demonstrate that they remain in our collective hearts. These pilgrimages are humbling journeys and weighty endeavors. Even so, one can't help but wish for a time with no new witness to bear.

The Bucks County Herald, October 15, 2015

We did travel to Oahu in November 2015. We wanted to see Pearl Harbor and the Arizona Memorial, which requires a short ride across the harbor on a small ferry. Our tour left at 10:30 a.m. on November 12. The prior day was totally booked as it was Veterans Day. Due to weather conditions and rough seas, we were the last tour of the day. We were leaving Oahu the next morning and were, therefore, especially grateful to have had the experience of this visit.

Our group heard a brief presentation, saw the wall of names, and like so many before us felt the emotional impact of our visit. Anyone who served on the Arizona may be buried at sea with their shipmates. A navy diver carries the urn of ashes as high as possible out of the water. When the ship is reached, they pause so that family and friends may pay their final respects. Then with a flip, the diver goes under and the urn is sucked through a portal into the ship's hull, to remain for eternity, mingling those ashes with the remains of their shipmates. As of November 2015, there were seven remaining veterans who may choose the USS Arizona as their final resting place.

USS Arizona Memorial, Pearl Harbor, Hawaii

Part Two:
Daily Life

"The secret of life is enjoying the passing of time."

JAMES TAYLOR

Frittering Away the Day

My horoscope this morning really calls me to task. "If you are more motivated to partake in inessential activities than you are in serious endeavors, don't expect to get anything important done. Try not to fritter away the day." I re-read it and ask myself, "Why?" In broad defiance of the oracles, I give myself permission to do just that. I make myself a cup of coffee and then remember to let the dog out. I rescue the daily paper from its puddle of water and hang it to dry on the ladder back chairs in the kitchen. Taking a sip of coffee, I start to unload the dishwasher.

Halfway through, I decide that some butternut squash soup would be good for dinner and begin to chop an onion. It simmers in the pan. Some apple would probably be a tasty addition, so I open the fridge and discover the center shelves are a mess and really should be wiped up. With a soapy dish sponge I begin scrubbing away only to realize the onions are beyond transparent, so I quickly add the chicken stock and squash chunks to boil.

I take a sip of coffee—it's now cold so I put it in the microwave. Then I remember the dog and the paper. While letting the puppy back in, I pick up a reasonably dry section of newspaper and read of others pursuing exploits great and small. I find myself unmoved.

The microwave beeps and I remember my coffee; on my way to get it I pause to check our iPad, a strategically placed diversion on the kitchen counter. My husband, who is out of town, remembers a check that needs to be sent. I wander into the family room, prepare the envelope and write the check. I return to the iPad and check my calendar to see if I've forgotten anything important. Yikes!! Where did the month go?? Yikes, I have an article to write!

The soup is progressing and I add the cream and chives. The phone rings and I agree to give blood for a local drive. The soup is now boiling and the cream has curdled, so I grab a whisk and stir hard to minimize the damage. Not quite smooth, but still tasty, so I consider it a saved situation and set the soup on simmer.

Walking through the dining room on my way to my office to write my article, I see a package containing capris that I received in the mail yesterday and decide to try them on. I take off the pants I have on, and proceed to the full-length mirror in my closet. They fit! I hang them up, feeling pleased with myself and my new purchase.

The doorbell rings, and l realize I don't know where I left the pants I was wearing. I peek out a window to see the mailman retreating after dropping off another package. I retrace my steps and still hear the microwave beeping and remember to (finally) get my coffee. But before I do, I finish unloading the dishwasher.

Then I grab the dog's leash and the envelope with the deposit check and take the dog with me to walk to a mail box. When I return, the microwave is still beeping, and I finally get my coffee, only to discover it has, once again, gone cold.

Finally, after much frittering, I sit at the table with a hot cup of coffee and a now dry newspaper. That's when I realize, after all my frittering, I've missed a meeting at church and a doctor's appointment!

September 2011

Too Many Choices

CLUTCHING MY ANCIENT BOTTLE OF aspirin, I let my eyes skip over the drugstore shelves. I need a replacement for the tired-looking specimen in my hand, which is of similar vintage to the cream of tartar on my spice rack. But, apparently, plain old aspirin doesn't exist anymore. The shelves are filled with a plethora of options: Low Dose, Advanced, Advanced Extra Strength, Safety Coated, Extra Coated, tablets, gel caps, lozenges, mini size, mega size—and on and on ad nauseam.

I feel a headache coming on. All I want is a bottle of plain old-fashioned no-frills aspirin. I leave the store in frustration, with no idea which of the available choices would provide the simple relief I seek.

A few days later, my husband goes to the supermarket for a few things and I ask that he pick up a box of my old standby, Kellogg's Special K with Protein. The phone rings. "They have Special K Original, Special K with Red Berries, Special K with Oats and Honey, Special K Multigrain, Special K with Vanilla Almond, Special K with Cinnamon Pecan, Special K with Fruit and Yogurt, Special K with Low Fat Granola, Special K with Blueberry and Special K with Chocolate Pieces."

He finishes this litany with a deep sigh and the wrong question, "Which one do you want?" I reminded him I'd asked for Special K with Protein. He reminds me that isn't one of the options offered. "Then you'll have to try a different supermarket," I say. *Silence.*

Psychologist Barry Schwartz, author of *The Paradox of Choice: Why More Is Less,* posits that while autonomy and freedom of choice are critical to our well-being, too many choices can paralyze rather than liberate. Schwartz's research indicates that when faced with an overwhelming number of choices, a vast majority of people will either end up unhappy with their choice, or make no choice at all.

One of the key rites of passage in becoming 65 is selecting our Medicare plans. Before I begin my rant, let me be clear—I truly value this earned benefit, and I would be remiss not to emphasize that the government options (Part A and Part B) are very straight-forward and simple.

Where the headache begins is with all the options offered by private insurers: Part C (Medicare Advantage, which combines Part A, B, and sometimes D—unless, of course, it doesn't), Part D (drug coverage of differing premiums and coverage), and the Med Supplements (for "gaps" not covered by original Medicare). Trying to keep it simple, I opt for Original Medicare and a Med Supplement.

For a Med Supplement, I get to choose from Plans A, B, C, D, F, F Select, G, K, L, M, and N—some of which may not be available in my state. As for which ones aren't available, it appears to be anybody's guess. Mercifully, Plans E, H, I, and J are no lon-ger available for sale. However, if one selects Part C, a Medicare Supplement policy (aka Medigap) isn't needed and can't be sold to you. Is everybody still with me? Ah, always the same old hands…

Remember Henry Ford's philosophy? We could have any color car we wanted, as long as it was black. It seemed the ultimate arrogance once, but these days it seems almost soothing. Granted, some choice is nice—but have things gone too far? From consumer products, to insurance plans, travel options, financial options, cable channels and more, Schwartz argues that eliminating consumer choices can greatly reduce anxiety (not to mention endless hours of Internet research trying to get enough information to make the "right" choice). Oxymoron aside, do we really need customized off-the-shelf products?

So what's a consumer to do? Schwartz's book offers some suggestions but, of course, each one comes with its own list of choices. I close the book. Now my head really hurts. Maybe I'll take a walk and get a cup of coffee. I enter the shop and a perky barista asks: "Small, medium, or large? Whole milk, skim, or soy? One shot or two? Hot or cold? Cinnamon or nutmeg?" I pause, awaiting my chance to enter her circling jump rope of options. She breathes. I pounce. "Would you by any chance have a plain old aspirin?"

The Bucks County Herald, May 15, 2012

Circles of Connection

I LOVE IT WHEN ONE aspect of life links with another—like little bubbles connecting to form an intersecting geodesic cluster. Many of these experiences are "six degrees of separation" phenomena: an acquaintance that went to the same college, a neighbor who grew up in the same town, a relative who once dated the spouse of a friend.

There are other kinds of connections as well. On my nightstand are several books. One of them is *Book of Ages: The Life and Opinions of Jane Franklin.* Jane was Benjamin Franklin's beloved younger

Thomas Cromwell

sister. I begin reading with anticipation. I am only four pages in when I am struck by references to a German blacksmith named Gutenberg, a minister to King Henry VIII named Cromwell, and a bookworm named Lady Jane Grey. The resonances from this one page reverberate in all sorts of directions:

My husband and I pull up our TV trays to watch a taped episode of Wolf Hall *while we savor our dinner and the history, intrigue and political maneuverings of—well, everybody in Henry VIII's court. The background story holds whispers and murmurs of Tyndale and his work of translating the Bible into English—further expanding the democratizing impact of Gutenberg's printing press—a major hinge of history. We relish the subtle beauty of actor Mark Rylance's performance as Thomas Cromwell, as well as the amazing story of Cromwell's rise from poverty and obscurity to wealth, power, and historical significance.*

An email alerts me that, Gutenberg's Apprentice, *a recent popular release, is available at the library. I rush to pick it up to learn about this irascible blacksmith and those who worked with him on a new device that could print multiple identical copies of any book. They chose to start with the Bible. Fast forward three centuries to colonial Boston where reading, writing, and the letterpress make their imprint on the family of Jane Franklin. As the craft transferred across the ocean from England to the colonies, the intuitive and inventive Franklins, especially Benjamin, leveraged its potential to gain wealth and fame. Pious Jane reads her Bible.*

Henry VIII's successor was his son Edward VI. As Edward lay dying, he named his freckle-faced, red-haired cousin Lady Jane Grey as his successor. He knew her to be learned and uninterested in idolatry—important attributes from the perspective of his time. Even as a teenager, Lady Jane eschewed the frivolity of life at court for the pleasures of a good book, whose company she preferred to that of any person. Her piety and learning were exceptional.

Lady Jane Grey

She reigned as Queen of England for a mere nine days before political events caught her in their swirl and she was escorted to the Tower of London to await her execution for high treason. As one of her final acts, Jane sent her sister a Bible—Tyndale's English translation—so that it might "teache you to live and learne you to die."

I'm picking up my grandchild at his home. On the kitchen counter rests a biography of Benjamin Franklin. My daughter-in-law enthuses about the amazing Ben and his inspirational rise from poverty and obscurity to wealth, power, and historical significance. Jane is not mentioned. As Ben tallied his wealth and accolades, she tallied her children.

In 1758, Ben Franklin made a pilgrimage to England to discover his familial roots. In rural Ecton, far from the Tower of London, he found his great-great-grandfather: a blacksmith and tinkerer named Thomas Francklyne. (Spellings of names and words changed frequently until the propagation of printing, which required standardization.) Thomas, after the death of Protestant Lady Jane Grey and during the reign of Catholic Queen Mary, invented an ingenious device that allowed him to read his Bible (in English) at will, but quickly hide it should there be an unexpected knock on the door. In 1565 Thomas Francklyne had a daughter. He named her Jane, a thinly veiled act of defiance. Jane might sound plain, but it was not just any name.

I attend a Bible study group where we read the scriptures together and discuss our reactions. We relate how the words impact each of us, based on who we are and what we have experienced in life. We argue, we debate, feel inspired or confused. We as individuals—not just our clergy—are left to wrestle with the beauties, ironies, and inconsistencies laid down in print. With accessibility to us all, we struggle with the scripture so that we may "learn how to live and how to die." We read, of course, in English. Our activity is conducted in plain sight and I note that not one of us is carted off for execution.

Thomas Francklyne's baby daughter Jane didn't live more than a month. We only know of her existence because the far-seeing Thomas Cromwell ordered every parish to keep a book of births, deaths, baptisms, and marriages. Without that imperative, Jane Francklyne would have been lost to the ages. Although she didn't live very long, her name reflected a certain rebellious spirit that ran in the family.

The name Jane was handed down through the generations and in 1712, in a new land an ocean away, Thomas Francklyne's great-great-granddaughter was born. Her father named her after the Nine Days Queen whose throne was a prison. He named her Jane. Everyone in the day was to learn to read—but not too much if you were a girl. Jane's brother Benjamin also taught her to write, an unseemly activity for a virtuous girl in the eighteenth century.

And so it goes. These looping ties and the circles of connectivity—like little bubbles of life—keep moving and intersecting, continually mingling elements of past, present and future. We were not created in a vacuum, nor do we live in one. We are connected by the myriad circles of life.

The Bucks County Herald, June 18, 2015

Techno-Avalanche

IT STARTED OUT SLOWLY. FIRST, I turned in my employer-provided ancient laptop and two-year-old smartphone. The holidays came, the year ended. And then, newly retired and blissfully ignorant, I confidently breezed into Staples to replace my old work tools with brand new ones. Filled with excitement, I bought a new computer. It was loaded with bells and whistles and even offered something called Windows Live which is in the Cloud, and sounded to me like PC heaven. I expected to plug in and immediately resume productivity.

Reality hit fast, cold, and hard. Initially I couldn't find my calendar (gasp), or my contacts (yikes), or even Word (oh no), because here's the thing—not only did I get a new computer, I also got a new operating system with a whole different logic and structure than what I had been using. I sat quietly and breathed deeply for a few minutes, and finally found Word. I wrote my first article and saved it with a big sigh of relief. And then I couldn't find it. It was somewhere in the Cloud… and PC heaven is so vast.

Since hard-copy manuals are a thing of the past, I ventured onto Online Help for answers: "If you'd like to know how to retrieve documents," it taunted, "**click here**." An obscure answer appeared. And then, "If you'd like to know more, **click here**." Then, "If you actually want an answer, **click here**." I plowed forward, hyperlinking my way deeper and deeper, slowly descending into PC hell.

Further adding to my anxiety was the barrage of pings and pop-ups announcing everything from a PC Store, to security, to support services. They asked probing questions like: "Do you want to purchase a device?" "Do you want to upgrade to 6.0?" "Do you have any idea what you're doing??" Even Internet Explorer popped up, wanting to tell me all about itself, and graciously offering "answers" such as "I don't know" or "Ask me later."

Deciding to change course, I went off to buy myself a smartphone. The sales person pirouetted through a dazzling display of options, complete with an endless waterfall of meaningless acronyms and features that made my head spin. I made a decision, but before I could actually buy the phone, I needed an email address, which, of course, I no longer had now that I'd retired. Happily, I was able to establish an email relatively easily, thereby restoring some sense of self-esteem and confidence.

On a roll, I plunged ahead to send out a few overdue messages. Unfortunately, I had failed to properly set up the account, so it wasn't saving "Sent" messages. Since there was no record, I assumed my messages didn't send. Doggedly I retyped and resent the same messages to the same people—over and over again. I have no idea how many people I alienated as a result.

It soon became a moot point, however, because when a new flock of perky pop-ups put me over the edge, I agreed to do whatever they asked, just to get them to stop. That's how I lost my Internet connection and so solved the problem of my manic email sending.

As if life wasn't complicated enough, I also traded in my vintage sedan for a beautiful new SUV. I soon realized I hadn't bought a car at all, but rather a big computer that goes places.* Additionally,

I received generous holiday gifts of a Kindle and an iPad, complete with new and different operating systems, online manuals and tutorials. Gradually, I'm figuring some things out; I've taken some courses, and may even resort to hiring a geek. In the meantime, I've come up with some very good answers when people ask me what I do all day now that I'm retired. I just smile and say, "I don't know." "Ask me later."

The Bucks County Herald, June 16, 2011

The March 7, 2016, issue of TIME *magazine features an article by Katy Steinmetz entitled "Forget the Distant Future, Smarter Cars are Already Here," where she reveals that modern cars have "more code than a Boeing 787"!*

Scam-Dalous

THERE'S SCAMMING, CRAMMING, SLAMMING, SPAMMING and phishing. If that's not enough, there's identity theft, financial theft, and medical and tax ID fraud. Hardly a day goes by when there's not at least one headline relating to a rip-off of one sort or another. Deceit is as old as the ages, but one might think that being reasonably cautious, reasonably educated, and reasonably savvy would offer protection. And it does—but only up to a point.

Financial guru Suze Orman is by any measure a smart, savvy, sophisticated woman whose rise from a waitress to a well-known author and financial entrepreneur is well known. And yet in her book, *The Courage to Be Rich*, she tells the story of how she made it big and then had to start all over because an employee came in one night and stole all her files, client contact names, computer programs and records—everything. It took three years and many court dates before she could resume her life. If it can happen to her, it can happen to anyone, so we must be alert. There are no silver bullets, but there are some good tips to help us protect ourselves. It makes me angry to be continually on red alert, but there it is.

In recent months, my inbox—with increasing frequency—has been hit with phishing emails posing as coming from well-known banks. They look very official, and contain website URLs and phone numbers that seem valid. The message, often with significant typos or syntax errors, is intended to alarm. The text goes something like this: "We have determined that [... different computers have logged on to your Online Banking account]; [multiple password failures have occurred on your online account]; [there has been an unusual level of activity on your account]"; and so on. Then the hook: "We need you to re-confirm your account information with us by clicking on the following link..." If you don't have an account with the bank, delete immediately. If it is your bank and you have not initiated the query, call your bank directly, using the number from your statement, to determine if there is a legitimate concern. Ask where to forward fraudulent emails.

Another ruse that really gets my goat is "urgent" early morning calls. One recent morning, a caller with a heavy foreign accent "alerted" us that our computer had been compromised and they needed us to log on right away, right away, right away so they could help us fix it. I was still somewhat sleepy so I had him repeat his request. "You must log on to your computer right away, right away, right away and type in this code I give to you." Suddenly the light bulb went on and I yelled, "How would you know anything about MY computer?!?!?" I hung up with a bang hoping to inflict pain. Urgency from an unknown caller is a big red flag.

Other "favorites" are email alerts that we've just won the lottery—in another country. How exciting! But did we ever buy a lottery ticket in another country? If that's not enough of a red flag, bells should go off when that nice man in Namibia tells us he only needs our bank account and social security number to make the transfer.

Scammers, of course, target the more vulnerable populations in our society, including young people, old people, and immigrants. As I age, I find it becomes ever more confusing and tiring to keep up with all the various ways the unscrupulous would violate us. It's not just the NSA that is tracking us.

I hate to be continually suspicious, yet the prevalence of deceit in our world demands caution. So I do the best I can. I read magazine articles, online tips, and financial institution and government flyers. It has helped me to identify quite a number of scams, and not fall prey—but alas, not all.

Last month, our credit card's fraud department sent an email and left a voice mail that our card had been compromised. We were urgently advised to call. Red alert! I didn't respond to the email or call the number left on our voice mail. Instead, I called the number from our current statement. I was quickly patched through to the fraud department where we established that I was indeed in Pennsylvania and not running up charges in Vancouver, British Columbia. The card was cancelled on the spot. Somewhere, somehow our number had been stolen, counterfeited, and put in use in Canada. Adding insult to injury, each Canadian charge generated foreign exchange fees. No matter what form it takes, it's all just plain scam-dalous!

The Bucks County Herald, August 21, 2014

"Oh Dem Silver Sneakers"

IN THE UNITED STATES WE traditionally celebrate and acknowledge a new year on January 1—the beginning of our Gregorian calendar year. In many ways, we also acknowledge and celebrate a new year in September. September is the beginning of the Jewish New Year and the new beginnings of a school year. In retirement, it is a time for many of returning home after a summer away, reconnecting with family and friends, and resuming activities. For me, it is also a birthday month, starting a new year of living life.

So, on September 1, I did what many (myself included) often do on January 1. I set goals and made resolutions. One of my retirement goals two Januaries ago was to get in shape and lose weight. I can't claim much progress and, indeed, often seem to be trending in the other direction. It isn't that I haven't tried—on three different occasions, I've lost (and ultimately regained) 10 pounds. But, even in my best Cleopatra-Queen-of-Denial mode, I have to acknowledge that losing 10 pounds three times really isn't the same as losing 30 pounds.

And yet, I am nothing if not persevering. So, on my "New Year's Day"—September 1—I once again called upon the good Dr. Atkins, and once again was rewarded with weight loss. This time, however, I wanted to add an exercise regimen as well. When the student is ready, the teacher appears. A Silver Sneakers card with my name on it arrived in the mail from my Medicare Supplement insurer. I was pleasantly surprised as I didn't anticipate this benefit, especially since my plan is the high-deductible variety. I decided this was a "sign" and soon visited one of the local participating fitness clubs to get started.

Flashback to my first day: there's a hubbub of confusion as the class gathers, people greet one another, grab props, and get set up. Others help me figure it all out. I stand next to my chair and gaze at my full-length reflection in the wall of glass behind the instructor. There's nothing like a full-length mirror to get one to truly face reality. It's a real call to action. I commit to improvement. Music blares, and we begin: legs marching, knees lifting, arms pumping. The unifying force of the beat replaces the chaos with a satisfying Rockettes-type precision. We look good!

The goal of the Silver Sneakers classes is not weight reduction per se. Rather it is to strengthen muscles, increase range-of-motion from head to toe, improve balance and coordination, and boost cardiovascular health. The program uses chair exercises, sitting and standing movement, weight resistance, band resistance, and bouncing balls of various colors. The instructor calls out to grab our balls for alternating hand tosses and bounces. Even the men laugh like school kids at the colorful mayhem which results as we bounce and throw the balls. Silver Sneakers is fun.

Silver Sneakers classes are done to music—great music: from Frank Sinatra to Petula Clark, the Beach Boys to The Beatles, and Marvin Gaye to Neil Diamond. We're encouraged to sing along if we wish. I'm sure our enthusiastic rendition of "Dooownntowwnnn" echoes all the way out into the parking lot. I don't know if the music has been selected because it's from "our era," or just because it's fun music with an infectious beat that makes everyone and anyone want to move. Either way—it works. I look in the mirror again, less concerned now with my body contours and more focused on faces. We're exercising facial muscles too—we're smiling.

Many times, a Zumba Gold class is included immediately following the Silver Sneakers workout. It's a real one-two punch—and sometimes it *does* double me over. But it is so much fun I hardly notice until the last cha-cha-cha. Zumba Gold, a modification of original Zumba, enhances the cardio element of the Silver Sneakers workout and the choreography further aids in coordination and balance. The choreography also requires one to focus and think. Ah, thinking! The brain needs strengthening too. Perhaps it's the endorphins, but by the time class ends, I'm starting to feel like the girl from Ipanema.

All this fun and health benefit as a result of an unexpected invitation to Silver Sneakers. All this exercise and work, yet I actually look forward to going. The struggle I've felt to get through other exercise classes is no longer an issue. These classes are joyful and fun—because basically, they're dancing—and I love to dance. I don't know what the outcome of my resolutions will be, but I do know I'm having fun—and feeling lighter. "Oh dem Silver Sneakers, oh dem Silver Sneakers—Silver Sneakers we love to wear because they look so neat." Yeah!

The Bucks County Herald, October 18, 2012

The Happy Cheapskate

When my husband and I were considering retirement, we both agreed we wanted to maintain the same lifestyle we enjoyed while working. This is quite a challenge now that we no longer have earned incomes. One of my favorite TV shows growing up was *I Remember Mama*. I'll never forget the episode when one of the children needed something and the parents gathered the family around to share ideas of how they could provide it without touching their savings account. The children, unafraid, approached the dilemma as a game—a puzzle to solve.

Of course, unbeknownst to the children, the unspoken "gotcha" was that there *was* no savings account—only resilience, creativity, and discipline. I have revisited the memory of that episode many times over the years, and it seems appropriate to revisit its lessons once again, to help us achieve our retirement goals. All we need to do is frame the current conundrum as a kind of puzzle to be solved—like a daily crossword—and, voila, drudgery and anxiety morph into a game. It is a fun game that keeps my antennae up, my mind active, and offers a kind of satisfaction similar to that of a golden nugget to a prospector. Allow me to share the wealth.

Always ask if there's a senior discount. You never know, and we've had some terrific surprises. Like a 50 percent discount in our waste management service, reduced rates on entertainment, and a lifetime pass to national parks which we have used coast-to-coast—from Acadia in Maine to Maritime National Park at Fisherman's Wharf in San Francisco. Also, a Medicare card provides not only health benefits, but other benefits as well. For example, flashing it at a Southeastern Pennsylvania Transit Authority (SEPTA) ticket window allows seniors to ride anywhere in Pennsylvania for only one dollar each way. A ten-strip reduces the price to 85 cents per ticket. Doesn't that bring a smile to your face, just thinking about it?

Reuse and Recycle. Jeff Yeager, author of *The Cheapskate Next Door*, espouses the philosophy of enjoying life more by spending—and accumulating—less. He has made "cheap" the new chic. In addition to countless personal finance tips, he reminds us of the environmental impact of our throwaway society. His practices and principles started me on the path down the Cheapskate Yellow Brick Road. You just have to admire a guy who can come up with 101 uses for used aluminum foil. My mother would be so proud. She was the ultimate recycler, decades before it was fashionable. My husband, who has serious "street cred" himself as a recycler, just shakes his head as he observes my mother's recycling habits manifest in my own.

Consignment Shops. Another way to reuse and recycle is via consignment shops. How wonderful it feels to be complimented on my Coach bag, leather jacket, Eileen Fisher outfit, and cute little chartreuse suede ballet flats, knowing that I've paid a fraction of what they would cost new. It's even more of a bargain if you can wait until the consignments go on half-price sale! And here's the best part. I pay for them with the money I earn by consigning my new and lightly-used but no-longer-relevant (that means they don't fit) clothes and accessories. Now you know that makes me happy!

This is all doubly true for grandchildren clothes. As every grandparent knows, children grow every time we turn around. Many consignment shops also carry children's clothes—many of which still carry their tags—giving testimony to the fact that children often outgrow their clothes before they've even had a chance to wear them.

Books are an expense item in our household too, so the used book store is also a real find. Many best sellers, children's books, and classics—among others—are available for a fraction of the retail cost. A consignment credit can be built here too for future purchases. Consigning clears away clutter and keeps our closets and shelves open for only the select "must haves." Purging definitely has an undeniable spiritual component as well, offering a new kind of freedom and lightness of being.

Consider membership in AAA and AARP. AAA isn't age based and offers savings to all who join. One can save on insurances and travel and roadside assistance. Our savings on these have more than paid our membership fee. Free TripTiks, apps, and guidebooks have enhanced our travels, and the variety of discounts and services are an asset.

If you are eligible for AARP, don't miss the chance to sign up. Many people, some only in their 50s, are insulted when they first receive the invitation to join. I encourage you to put umbrage aside and give AARP a chance. Their financial, health, travel, entertainment and retirement tips and/or discounts can net your household thousands of dollars you may have otherwise not received or saved.

For example, a divorced friend of mine, who was married over 10 years and never remarried, didn't realize she might be eligible to receive Social Security based on her ex-husband's benefit—whether he had started drawing benefits or not and without any diminishment to his benefit. I showed her an article from AARP. She now receives much-needed additional support for her self-employment income and can hold off taking her own benefit until she turns 70. That's real money. AARP provides magazines and online bulletins with solid information on retirement issues, product and service discounts, travel information, relevant book and movie reviews and social advocacy. (Yes, they are a powerful lobby on behalf of seniors.) Membership is nominal and the benefits more than exceed the cost.

Being a cheapskate in certain circumstances is a contributor to living the lifestyle we want in retirement. It's worth every penny—and a fun challenge too.

The Bucks County Herald, September 20, 2012

The Blame Game

Toward the end of World War I, both Allied and German newspapers celebrated victories—real or imagined. But after four years of battle, the loss of over 700,000 soldiers, starving citizens at home and in the trenches, and no appreciable gains from a major last-ditch offensive, the German general of infantry, Erich Ludendorff, called for an armistice. It was signed November 11, 1918.

Soon after, a right-wing journal in Germany started blaming not Austria, not France, not Russia, not Britain, not Germany, not the kaiser or the tsar, nor the military advocates. No. It blamed the Jews and socialists. This was nonsense. It didn't matter. Rather than the governments and their advisors acknowledging the senseless destruction they had wrought, and working on ways to prevent future wars, most chose to find someone else to blame. The Jews and socialists became improbable but convenient scapegoats. This was not harmless. The repetition of the lie led to people believing the lie and we all know how this ended 20 years later: Heil Hitler. Blaming may delay consequences—but there are always consequences.

The psychology of blame is not new—it's been with us since Adam and Eve. (She made me do it!) In his 2010 book, *The Blame*

Game, author Neil Farber, MD, PhD, moves his reader through the stages from blaming to personal responsibility with humor and insight. The blame game manifests on stages both large and small. We knock over someone's drink: not our fault! Why did that person put their glass where we might bump it? Students not doing well in school? Blame the parents! Blame the teachers! Really good blamers blame both. Having a bad day at the office? Blame the boss. Unless you are the boss. In that case, blame the employees. In his book's preface, Farber notes that if you don't like the name of his book or its contents, it's not his fault!

Today we are suffering no end of US presidential candidates who are having a field day "telling it like it is" and garnering much support as they blame immigrants and minorities in general, and Mexicans and Muslims in particular, for any given woe that America does now or has ever experienced. Selective amnesia serves as a magic wand allowing them to wipe clean their foreign ancestries that ultimately led to their US citizenship. Effective marketing is making the shameful seem refreshing.

Ironically, the US states most vehement about Mexican immigrants and the need to build a border wall with Mexico don't seem to remember that they once were Mexico. But it's much easier to receive cheers for playing an adolescent blame game, than to seriously work toward real solutions to a complex issue.

Not to be outdone by US pols, President Xi Jinping of China just declared that the current crash in the Chinese economy has been caused by the Dalai Lama and Tibetan Separatists. A bemused Dalai Lama is quoted as responding: "All I do is meditate and pray. I barely read the newspaper." Everyone, it seems, needs a scapegoat, no matter how ridiculous.

Speaking of walls, another of our illustrious presidential wannabes has said a wall on the US/Canada border—the longest international border in the world—is worth considering. Perhaps he thinks it will keep out cold northerly winds or even the contagion of successful socialized medicine?

As a former resident of Buffalo, New York, I spent frequent day trips and weekends in Canada to enjoy dinner, sightseeing, theater, baseball games, wine tastings, shopping and more. It's a nice place. If the philosophies and faux solutions offered by a presidential candidate should prevail, a wall with Canada might make sense indeed—to keep US citizens in the US.

If the current political rhetoric is a true indicator of who we've become as a nation and as Americans, many of us might consider fleeing to our civilized neighbor to the north. And if we did? Well who could blame us?

The Bucks County Herald, September 17, 2015

Part Three: Inspiration

"If you are always trying to be normal,
You will never know how amazing you can be."

Maya Angelou

Room with a View

MY LORD, WHAT A MORNING! Nature has opened her arms and gently dropped a still, silent snow, creating a winter wonderland where branches and boughs are outlined with sharp clarity even as they are softened and quieted. Sunlight glints off the crystalline flakes, creating a diamond-encrusted world. I am entranced by the beauty and the silence.

I might not find this all so wonderful if, in fact, I wasn't eight days into retirement. No need to worry about getting to work, no need to search for boots, no need to do anything except snuggle deeper under the covers. And when I did finally arise—it was glorious.

Week One of retirement was tough. Initially I thought it was because I felt purposeless. On reflection, I realize I felt too busy! All my body wanted to do that first week was sleep and read, but my mind was still in work mode and felt compelled to fully implement all my retirement plans at once. After all, I was retired—time to get busy!!

My natural goal orientation was working against me. I entered Week Two much the wiser, giving myself permission to move more gradually, albeit still as a seeker.

A few years ago, I reconnected with an old friend. We were enjoying catching up when she told me that one of her first memories of me, from some 30 years ago, was my desire to be a published writer. I was stunned when she told me; stunned because I had actually told someone, and stunned because I had tucked it so far back in my mind, I had almost forgotten. But she did not.

Sometimes we aren't the ones who keep our dreams alive. Sometimes the flame is kept alive by others on our behalf until we're ready to pursue it.

My "career" began as a checkout girl at Woolworth's when I was 15 years old. I have probably *thought* about retirement ever since. But I didn't start actually *planning* for it until a few years ago. My friend's recollection started me strategizing on how I could actually achieve my dream in retirement.

Virginia Woolf once said that to write, a woman has two important needs: money and a room of her own. I am happy to say that my work life has ended better than it began, and I have been blessed with a lucrative and fulfilling vocation in the latter part of my career. Having remarried at the age of 60, I also have a partner to share the load.

Next I needed a room of my own and, two years before my projected retirement date, construction began on a small addition off the master bedroom that houses my writing nook—and a walk-in closet. Not all my dreams are career-related. There's a skylight above me, a very long double-hung window to my west, and a wall of sliding glass doors that face north, overlooking the new deck that completed the project.

When I sit at my desk—or in nice weather, when I'm out on the deck—I overlook a wooded lot filled with crimson cardinals and a bevy of other birds. It makes me feel as if I am in a tree house—my own little writer's aerie.

This morning, as I sat down to write, I first gave myself time to just enjoy the beauty of last night's snowfall and give thanks for all the reasons I had the opportunity to do so. My little sanctuary is a wonderful space and a lovely perk as I work toward the fulfillment of my dream to become a writer.

January 2011

Pursuing our Dreams

I HEARD THE VIDEO BEFORE I saw it. It was filled with a determined wind and the noisy flapping of brightly colored prayer flags. My husband was standing 18,192 feet above sea level, high above Nepal's Khumbu Glacier on a peak named Kala Pathar, panning the vista with his camera, capturing the dramatic outline and cragginess of this giant massif from one of the best vantage points in the Himalaya. Sitting on the border between Nepal and Tibet, it is called Sagarmatha, "The Head in the Great Blue Sky," in Nepali, and Chomolungma, "Goddess Mother of the World," in Tibetan. We call it Mt. Everest—the world's tallest peak.

My native son of Kansas has loved mountains as long as he can remember and has felt an affinity for them that he cannot explain. But he knows they are in his soul. Relatively recently along the path of life, he decided he would like to trek the Himalaya—to see some of the highest mountains in the world, most especially Mt. Everest. His vision did not contain a desire to summit Everest ("I don't have a death wish," he explains), but he did want to see it, up close and personal, which is still a significant physical, mental, and spiritual challenge.

I remember years ago reading a poem called "I Dreamed I Was a Ballet Dancer." A young woman describes her longing to be a

ballet dancer, but she had to get up really early to practice, and the toe shoes really hurt, the rehearsals were really hard, and so she just pulled up the covers and went back to sleep to dream her dream… but never to achieve it.

Some dreams die slow. Some dreams die hard. Some dreams die aborning. Some dreams just gradually fade away. And some dreams are actually achieved, if one has the time and the commitment. For my husband, retirement provided the time, and the strength of his dream provided the commitment and passion.

To trek several miles a day in the Himalaya, carrying a day-pack, up steep ascents and down rocky inclines, one needs to be in top physical condition. My husband has always maintained a good workout schedule, but he knew that to achieve Everest Base Camp—and hopefully to peak Kala Pathar for the optimal Everest sighting—he would need to ramp it up considerably. His full conditioning began during the summer in the Rocky Mountains, where he gradually increased the length and rigors of his climbs, breaking in his new boots and other hiking gear and, of course, carrying a fully-loaded daypack. He joined a local hiking club, where the leaders set a challenging pace.

One day he determined he was ready to hike a "fourteener," as the highest Colorado peaks are called. He achieved his goal, but found the ascent challenging, especially as he encountered the ever thinning air at the higher altitudes. He wondered if he had bitten off too much; wondered about the wisdom of trying such a physical challenge at this stage of life. But he didn't pull the covers up and go back to sleep. He kept at his routine, and a couple of weeks later ascended two more "fourteeners"—in the same day! His efforts were paying off and his confidence returned.

When we returned home, he continued his conditioning, expanding his standard workout to two hours a day. He worked at it every day—even though it was really hard; even though he got really tired. As he finalized his packing and we prepared to leave for the airport for his flight to the exotic ports of Bangkok and Kathmandu, he felt he had done all he could to prepare himself.

He also knew his preparation, albeit necessary, was no guarantee that his goals would be achieved. The mountains are to be respected. Sometimes in spite of the best conditioning, other factors such as the food, sleeping conditions, weather, water, altitude, and so on, ad nauseam (sometimes literally), can debilitate a trekker, or thwart the dream. Trekkers may make it to Base Camp or Kala Pathar, only to find the great monolith shrouded in clouds, totally hidden from view. Some may not make it that far.

Of the five trekkers who started the journey with my husband, two had to descend to lower altitudes before reaching their goal— one was carried by Sherpas in the middle of the night, so dire was the altitude sickness. Another wasn't sleeping well and was frightened of having the same fate, and went down voluntarily with a guide the next day. A third had to be stabilized in the portable Pressurized Altitude Chamber (PAC), before being allowed to continue. It was bitterly disappointing.

But even if we don't achieve our dreams, our pursuit can still hold value. Even if our summit attained is lower than we dreamed, sometimes the valleys also hold incredible beauty; sometimes the "almost highest" peaks still provide a thrill; sometimes we learn much about ourselves and others, even as we descend. At least if we try, we won't waste time agonizing over "what if" and "if only..."

The remaining hikers were by far the oldest of the group: a 66-year-old woman from Los Angeles, and my 65-year-old husband. They both reached Base Camp and Kala Pathar under their own steam, in bright sunshine and under blue skies. Viewing Everest from this vantage and with such clarity was an exhilarating experience—one which could not be assumed but which gloriously exceeded expectations. My husband was fortunate—he achieved his dream and more—gaining profound personal and spiritual experiences all along the way, as well as the thrill of attaining Base Camp and the view of Chomolungma from Kala Pathar.

People ask me if he has inspired me to do a similar trek. No, no, and no. He has, however, done something more important than that. He has inspired me to identify and pursue my own dream. Perhaps he will do the same for you.*

The Bucks County Herald, November 17, 2011

Since climbing to Everest Base Camp and Kala Pathar in 2011, Steve has trekked Patagonia in 2014 and the Haute Route in Europe from Chamonix, France, to Zermatt, Switzerland, in 2016. He has climbed many mountains in his beloved Colorado including several "fourteeners."

Becoming a Master

WITH THE SWIFTNESS OF THE Niagara cataract heading toward the Falls, we have blitzed through one year and jettisoned into another. Were we not just keening in anguish over Y2K and its untold potential for destruction? And yet here we are 13—13!—years later, survivors of both a new millennium and a supposed Mayan apocalypse.

Once again we have a new year—a clean slate upon which to reflect on the previous year, a clean slate upon which we may attempt to revise or amend the past and create the future. In the opening essay of the "On the Road" section of this book, I cite business guru David Ulrich, recalling a seminar in which he highlighted his key areas of focus for personal development: the Physical, the Emotional, the Social, the Intellectual and the Spiritual. A year later, I quoted theologian and philosopher Meister Eckhart. It appears I have made a shift. Eckhart asks us what we would do if we felt most secure. He's encouraging us to identify what we *want*; he is drawing us into discernment.

In preparation for the new year, I read *Master Class* by Peter Spiers, a graduate of Harvard College, the London School of Economics, and the Tuck School of Business Administration at Dartmouth, and now an executive with Road Scholars (formerly

Elder Hostel). Ever the underachiever, Spiers soon launched a study of participants in the Road Scholars programs to determine how they maintained vigor and achievement in their 60s, 70s, 80s, and beyond.

Spiers found a variety of similar activities among the respondents, which he classified into four key dimensions and christened "The Master Way of Life." The dimensions are *Socializing, Moving, Creating, and Thinking.* These resonate with Ulrich's key areas, with one exception: Spiers' survey results do not overtly mention faith, discernment, or "the Spiritual." His focus is on achievement—and he doesn't mean getting up before 9:00 a.m. or successfully locating the car keys.

Not that there's anything wrong with achievement. It has certainly been important to me along the way, and in many behaviors I'm still as Type A as I've always been. However, I am noticing incremental changes as I continue to march deeper into my 60s. The word "achievement" now makes me feel tired, pressured, and societally judged. I've come to prefer the word "fulfillment." "Fulfillment" feels calming, expansive, personal, and…spiritual. Achievement feels external; fulfillment feels internal.

In fairness to Spiers, he makes some excellent points, and suggests a variety of activities—supported by solid research—that promote cognitive health, vitality, and contribution as we age. His self-led course of instruction guides us through 31 (count 'em!) specific activities so that we, too, can become a Master—i.e., someone who is living a balanced life by juggling—ahem, *balancing*—these 31 activities.

One can also receive credit for independent study, should one somehow be able to squeeze it in. Participants are to track activities on a Credit Tracking Chart and assign points to each activity. To pass from Master Class 101 to 201, 301, and ultimately 401, the participant must achieve a certain minimum number of points. If participants make it to completion, they become "true Masters."

The thought of the whole endeavor exhausts me. Clearly Spiers himself is on a fast track, but it strikes me he may have conflated all activities by all participants in the study to come up with these recommendations. Taking time to smell the flowers doesn't seem to be among them.

I have no aspirations to become a Master. Zero. Zilch. None. I haven't stopped *Socializing, Moving, Creating, and Thinking*, but I've adopted an "all things in moderation" approach. There was a time when I may have welcomed Spiers' highly-structured syllabus. A time when maybe I would have aspired to tracking and adding up all my points and becoming a true Master. But now—here at the beginning of a new year—it frankly feels *so* "yesterday."

The Bucks County Herald, January 17, 2013

Autumn "NUTS"

KA-PLINK, KER-PLOP, KA-BANG. I SIT at the kitchen table, nicely nestled into a sunny bay window which affords a good view of the backyard. I listen to the recurring autumnal symphony provided by acorns dropping from the oak trees that surround our home. Squirrels scurry and scamper, each rushing to stuff its cheeks with as many nuts as possible, before another does. They are in all-out winter preparation mode and these sounds foretell a bumper crop. I marvel at the squirrels' efficiency and purposefulness, especially as contrasted to my lack of either.

Even the oracles of astrology seem to have noticed. One daily horoscope cautions: "It's important for you to remain organized. You have so much going on right now that you need to stay focused." I'm not sure what I have going on, but I agree I need to regain some focus and get organized. The other horoscope is less kindly: "If you are more motivated to partake in inessential activities than in serious endeavors, don't expect to get anything important done." Ouch! Ouch! Ouch! That was direct.

Dr. Oz, the charismatic TV host, was quoted in a recent AARP article: "… Among the major stressors in our lives are Nagging Unfinished Tasks (NUTs)." Unlike acorns, these NUTs collect in the back of our minds, generating anxiety and sucking energy and focus from our days. Of course, in retirement, it's nice to have some leeway to meander, and not move as quickly as we once did. But I'm starting to realize that since we've returned from our cross-country trip this summer, I'm feeling somewhat overwhelmed and rudderless. Could it be because of an ever accumulating basket of NUTs?

We all have them, of course, and they never totally go away—even as one is checked off the list, another is forming. But after a summer away, I seem to have accumulated more NUTs than usual. All the ones I left behind in July are still there, plus all the ones that accumulated over the summer. Even more have gathered since our return home. And the more they pile up, the more I seem to stumble upon distractions (aka "inessential activities") that have become barriers to truly accomplishing anything. Unlike the squirrels', my bumper crop of NUTs feels more burden than bounty.

I consider Dr. Oz's caution about not confronting our NUTs and realize that my dallying is no longer feeling good; rather, it's a form of denial and escape from my growing anxiety. My horoscope is right! I DO need to get focused and I do need to stop directing so much effort into non-essential activities. I'm unused to a summer off and realize I've totally lost any kind of rhythm to my days. I still want to have time to linger over coffee at the kitchen table, but I don't like the niggling anxiety that's starting to arise. As I continue to transition into retirement, I am starting to understand the need to consciously re-create the structure of my days and life so that I deal with the NUTs, while still accommodating my desire for time to just "be." It is autumn—a good time to get back on track, prioritize what needs to be done, clean up my office work area, break tasks down into their components, make some lists and start making some progress, little by little, one day at a time. To do otherwise would just drive me, well...NUTS!

The Bucks County Herald, October 20, 2011

The Creative Process

Gooooooooooood morning! Gooooooooooood morning! Like a clarion call, the booming voice sang—yes *sang* this diplomatic, but still emphatic, call to order. Participants stopped their chatter, quickly topped off their coffees, grabbed another pastry and selected a seat. The chairs were arranged in the round in the middle of a reception/performance area surrounded by art and antiquities. We could see each others' faces as the co-leaders laid out the goals and process for the day.

Perhaps it was the recent hint of warmth, the sighting of precocious buds, or other harbingers of spring—our perennial cue for regeneration and rebirth—that reminded me of this experience in creative process from last November. The session was exploratory, to develop ideas of how to best utilize the unique surroundings provided by the Mercer Museum in Doylestown, Pennsylvania. Participants came from Pennsylvania, New Jersey, New York, and one even from Hawaii (at least originally).

There were actors and authors and poets and musicians, sound technicians, technology gurus—and one slightly out-of-her-league lifestyles columnist. Each brought a unique perspective. Each was committed to the process and invested in creating a special outcome. I was honored to have been included.

A brief introduction to the museum, and a review of the goals of world traveler and collector Henry Mercer, was provided by the vice president of collections and interpretation. The vice president's overarching goal is to keep reinventing the way the museum is used, thereby encouraging people to see the galleries with new eyes. His specific goal was the development of a storytelling event to draw existing visitors, as well as new seekers—those who might not otherwise come there—to experience and explore this remarkable place. Our goal was to develop a concept that would be implemented into a performance experience. He wanted something that contained audio, visual, and kinetic elements.

We were divided into four groups and invited to wander the heights and depths of this large, gray concrete castle. As if we were roaming through an Escher print, we climbed secret stairways leading to "hidden" rooms, found paw prints from long ago, and viewed fellow participants at other levels and angles across the immense space. We reacted to the items around us, mostly in positive ways, although a member of our group was overcome by the top floor's display of gallows and implements of torture.

One man in our group zeroed in on a milking stool. He told the group how it illustrated the Japanese concept of *wabi-sabi*, in which the animate nature of inanimate objects is conveyed—the ways in which the object's history, shape, and markings indicate human ownership and human lives. As we moved through the exhibits, we discovered a small room with an entire wall covered in tiles. While some were simple decorations, others represented stories, from the Bible to local life. Fingers caressed the tiles, reading the tales by touch as well as by sight. In the sewing section quilts were discussed, noting how every patch represented a story of the community and individual lives within it.

When we reconvened to discuss reactions and brainstorm ideas, many participant memories emerged. One man remarked that the swords and weapons gallery reminded him of gifts given to him by a friend of his parents. He had proudly displayed them in his boyhood room and savored the reminder. An African American woman talked about the tortoise shell combs and other hair ornaments and how they evoked for her the challenges inherent in hair of African descent. The many and varied containers throughout the collection brought a comparison to stories, and it was noted that complex ideas can often be "contained" or remembered through story.

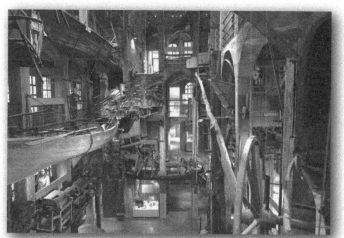

Photograph courtesy of the Mercer Museum, Doylestown, Pennsylvania
Image: Interior Photograph of the Mercer Museum

Everyone agreed these were tools and implements that helped to build a nation as well as individual lives and communities. These items illuminated an evolution in history and humanity that is universal across many cultures. It was noted how beautiful many of the items were and how hard it was to resist touching or picking them up. One participant was inspired to create a poem. The surrounding artifacts murmured to her, creating a buzz in her consciousness and eliciting an emotional response and connection to those who had gone before.

Museums everywhere are rediscovering narrative. They want to discern and present the stories in their collections and relate them to the contemporary visitor. This autumnal experience of creative process was, by design, a communal, collegial event intended to harness the generative power of collective minds. The goals of the day were not to answer all the questions, but to start the journey of how to interact with the collection, to develop a performance that would make it new and relevant. To resurrect it, if you will. It was a visceral and evocative process and it reminded me that even in the heart of autumn or winter, we can still experience spring.

The Bucks County Herald, April 16, 2015

Discernment

THIS MONTH REPRESENTS MY FIRST anniversary as a features writer for a local newspaper. It is a pleasure for me to share this occasion with all readers and to thank you for your interest and hospitality. My first article revolved around a quote from French pilot and philosopher, Antoine de Saint-Exupéry. In observing an accountant preparing to leave his post for the Spanish Civil War, Saint-Exupéry muses: "Sergeant, Sergeant, what will you do with this gift of life?" It is a quote that has stayed with me ever since I read it over 30 years ago. Perhaps that is why one of my male readers refers to my column as an exercise in French existentialism.

Wikipedia offers that the existential attitude is characterized by a sense of disorientation and confusion in the face of an apparently meaningless or absurd world. That doesn't really fit my drift. Kierkegaard, often regarded as the father of existentialism, maintained that the individual is solely responsible for giving his or her own life meaning and for living that life passionately and sincerely in spite of many obstacles. Not bad.

But my own interpretation feels quite different. It is definitely theistic in nature, and while it may include some anxiety and angst, that is not what defines it. Rather my intent is to offer a voice focused on the baptismal notion of *discernment*. Discernment is not easy work and often, in fact, contains anxiety and angst. But discernment is not defined by it. Webster's defines "discernment" as "the power or faculty of the mind by which it distinguishes one thing from another; acuteness of judgment; power of perceiving differences of things or ideas; insight; acumen; as, 'the errors of youth often proceed from the want of discernment.'" Boy, can I relate to that!

For me, though, discernment is more. It is God's pull on our psyches. Its goal is to help us manifest the fullest possible version of ourselves, to identify and utilize our individual gifts in ways that contribute to our world, and to aid and abet our response to the call of our soul.

My understanding of discernment as it pertained to a vocation or career didn't manifest until I was in my 30s. My career guidance around the kitchen table consisted of a single sentence. "Get a good job with Philco; they'll take care of you for the rest of your life." Unlike Saint-Exupéry's sergeant, any questioning on my part was rendered unnecessary. There's a real seduction to having such answers provided for us—but some key limitations as well. Philco, for all its post-World War II prominence, didn't survive the '60s as a corporate entity—and who knows if I would have been hired anyway? So as an adult, newly divorced with two young children, I started thinking about what path I should follow. I had no idea.

Just as I was feeling a little desperate, my church offered some hope in the form of a weekend retreat called, "Thank God It's Monday." I jumped at it. The crux was about finding work that aligned our gifts and talents with different kinds of work. It was about considering why we are incarnate and what our calling—our vocation—might be. It was about trying to align making a living with enjoying a life. It was overwhelming and exciting all at once. Some people know their vocation from an early age. Many others of us—most of us?—have more of a struggle and ongoing process. How many times did I throw back my head and yell, "Dear Lord, just tell me what you what me to do!"

Teilhard de Chardin wrote a beautiful letter to an impatient nephew describing the "slow work of God." I happened to discover it at an important juncture. Yes, I needed to make money, but I also started to feel the pull of an evolutionary process and felt an unseen hand guiding me step-by-step. Eventually, I did arrive at a place where I wanted to shout, "Thank God it's Monday." My path or "career" (from the Latin "carrier," meaning a vehicular road or highway) was an arduous one, and ultimately required that I lose my job to move forward. But in the end, every twist in the road led to my vocation: a role as a career consultant for a human resources consulting firm. It was as close to God's work in the world as I have ever known,* and in retrospect it showed me that support always surrounds us—even when it doesn't feel like it. Sometimes we just have to trust the slow work of God.

Now that I am retired, discernment has taken on a new dimension. Retirement has afforded me the option of exploring dimensions of my vocation previously unavailable when the focus was the necessity of earning money. Now, my focus can be more about living life—more about "acuteness of judgment and understanding" as Webster would say. What is it that I am to do with this gift of both life AND retirement? Who am I now? (I do feel like a very different person.) How do I think of myself and how do I present myself?

At the risk of being obvious, I have arrived at the place where Virginia Woolf says one needs to be to be a writer. Thanks to Social Security, I have money of my own; thanks to starting my retirement discernment a few years ahead of the actual event, I also have a room of my own—a small addition off the master bedroom with lots of light and a window overlooking a wooded lot. It's been a dream deferred for many years and I'm grateful to be given the gift of pursuing it now.*

Nonetheless, it has been a transition. I laugh to think of how my confusion presented itself. One day I noticed that Staples was offering 100 free business cards. Great. This was just the opportunity to develop a new business card to align with my new identity. The staff person at Staples started showing me the design options and initially I spotted one that was linear, tailored, pretty darn corporate looking. Then, as we continued to scan the options, I noticed one that looked very artistic, like scribbling—PERFECT for a new writer! In the end I decided to use them both. When I got the finished product I was horrified. "Dear Lord," I thought, "I'm schizophrenic!" And in a way, I think I truly was…caught in process between two very different worlds. I have another card now, with just one theme. Apparently I'm settling down a little…

OK—so discernment is important. But it wouldn't be fair to leave readers all alone with no GPS. So, here are actions that have aided me in this process. Hopefully they will affirm and assist your own discernment process as well:

Ask yourself questions. As a career consultant, I used to encourage my clients to draw a pie of life and identify the "slices" as they currently exist. In another pie, I encouraged them to arrange the size and labels of the slices as they would want them to be.

Another technique is to pretend you've won the lottery. After a year on the beach, what's next? Meister Eckhart encourages us to do exactly what we would do if we felt most secure, which leads to the question, if I felt most secure (financially, emotionally, socially) what would I do? Now that's pro*voca*tive! (Notice the embedded term *vocare* meaning "to call"!)

Listen to your words. How many times a day does the word "should" enter your vocabulary? How different would your actions be if you substituted "want" for "should"? How would the substitution of one little word potentially alter your day?—your life?

Listen to your body. Does your body fill with energy around particular endeavors? And does it feel cobbled with ball and chain for others? Sometimes we start down a path that initially feels good, but increasingly becomes a slog. Kenny Rogers' song "The Gambler," counsels the importance of knowing "when to hold," and "when to fold." Our bodies hold keys of wisdom.

Read. Well, of course, I'd say this, right? What else would a writer say? One exercise I suggested to clients was to go to a good bookstore and scan the magazine rows. What draws you? What makes your skin crawl? Now move to the book aisles and do the same thing. It's not scientific, but it can be enlightening. Ask yourself why you enjoy a particular book—what draws you and keeps you hooked to the end? Ask yourself what you have learned—about the topic and yourself.

Network. You've heard it recommended as a job search tool, but it is so much more. At bottom, it is a type of research and is indispensable in discernment. As you talk with and learn about others, you inevitably learn about yourself.

Hibernate. Become bear-like in the winter. Although not my favorite season, it does have its advantages. So bundle up, sit back, relax and enjoy the opportunity to move a little slower. I know— that's naïve in a world with PCs, cell phones, families, work, etc. If you can't carve out the season, try to carve out some hibernation time within each day or week. And as you do, let insights and impressions come to you without trying to draw them.

In the pursuit of our purpose, let us not forget to relax and enjoy the process and where we are right now. As Bobby McFerrin reminds us, "Don't Worry—Be Happy." God will guide and God will provide—especially if we make space in our lives to hear the messages. To everything there is a season, and a time to every purpose under heaven. Instead of viewing winter, or other slow times, with discontent, view them as opportunities for discernment. If not now, then when?

The Bucks County Herald, January 2012

°In an interesting twist of fate, as I enter my 70s I am returning to work with my former employer to continue to do career management work, but on an as needed basis. I am also continuing to pursue my career as a writer and author with the publication of this book. After sifting through decades of different endeavors and false starts, I now find myself pursuing two satisfying vocations. I did not see that coming!

Part Four:
Family Ties

"Your heart and my heart are very old friends."

HAFIZ

Miracles upon Miracles

"HE'S HERE!" MY SON JUBILANTLY announced. I hang up the phone and rush out the door to pick up my husband at work, grateful he can get away on this momentous day. And also grateful to have someone else drive as I am too emotional to safely make the journey across state lines. We finally arrive at the hospital. As I enter the room, my smiling son walks toward me and places a bundle in my arms. Even through my tears of joy, I can see how totally beautiful and perfect is this child—my first biological grandchild* and our first grandson. I say a silent prayer of thanks for his and his parents' well-being. This most common of events is still a miracle each and every time.

What is it about grandparenting that makes it so special? Perhaps as parents our marveling was distracted by the business of making a living and keeping up with all the minutiae of running a household and caring for a young family. I know that as a parent I didn't feel I had the luxury to sit and marvel every time one of my children yawned or ate a Cheerio.

Grandparenting is different. For us it is intermittent, allowing the joy without the weight of day-to-day care, tantrums, or diarrhea from one end to the other. This intermittency allows us to simply be with the child and push other demands to the side until later. It also creates a time warp. Seeing progress weekly or monthly is different from seeing it daily. It's more startling, more amazingly crystalline because the change isn't blurred by incremental progress.

Suddenly (to us), they are holding up their heads, rolling over, crawling, eating "real" food, walking, gurgling incoherently—then in the blink of an eye—talking, laughing, and calling us by name. Oh the joy of it all. I am finding every cliché about grandparenting to be true.

More subtly, grandparenting may also be an opportunity for redemption. An opportunity to hopefully be the grandparent we always wanted to be, even if we sometimes fell short in being the parent we wanted to be. An opportunity to apply whatever wisdom and understanding we have gained as we matured. Two years ago, I could not have imagined the recent hospital scene. Two years ago, almost to the day, my son had estranged himself from us and cut off all communication and all contact for almost a year. It broke my heart.

But things change—and that same son now walked toward me beaming with joy as he placed his hours-old child in my arms. Based on where things were such a relatively short time ago, this too was a miracle. I am supremely grateful. I am also reminded how often we may need to take the long view as we wait for the universe to manifest our deepest desires. I rejoice in once again being invited into his life in an integral way and in sharing the joy of this new child. Miracles upon miracles—woven from the events of everyday life. Some things truly are worth the wait.

The Bucks County Herald, March 24, 2011

Three years later, this same son and his wife blessed us yet again; this time with a precious granddaughter. See "I'm Having a Baby Sistah!" also in this section.

The Baptism

PARISHIONERS AND GUESTS MURMUR AS they settle into the pews. Soft colors emanate from the large stained glass window in the north wall, suffusing the chapel with a muted glow. In the front pew, my son and daughter-in-law wrestle my grandson into his father's christening dress—the same gown I made for my older son some 40 years ago. My younger son, flown in from New Mexico to offer his commitment as a godparent, sits beside them.

A bell sounds, creating a hush, and a Bach voluntary dramatically swells from the organ and fills this small, beautiful space.

The service of the Feast of Pentecost and the Celebration of the Sacrament of Holy Baptism has begun.

My mind strays as I reflect on the importance—and challenge—of this sacrament, which speaks directly to our responsibility to discern our purpose in this life. Why have we been made incarnate? What is it we are to do now that we are here? What are our gifts and how will we use them? The epistle is from the First Letter of Paul to the Corinthians (12:3b-13)... *"Now there are varieties of gifts, but the same Spirit...To each is given the manifestation of the Spirit for the common good..."*

I think about my renewed struggle to determine my gifts and how they might be applied in this world. Discernment can be so daunting. I reflect how God's hand—sometimes not so gently—gradually led me to a path that resulted in my work as a career consultant. It was not a conscious goal on my part, but I recognized it as one manifestation of God's work in this world, and felt privileged to serve in this way.

I wonder now, in retirement, what new vocation (*vocare* from the Latin "to call") might be in store for me. I wonder why I even think that something *is* in store! And yet, I do. I've mercifully stopped trying to force a resolution and, uncharacteristically for me, have decided to opt for an organic emergence of what God's purpose for me might be in this encore phase.

I think about my sons and their oh-so-different paths. My older son, with his drive and entrepreneurial spirit, has built a viable business and achieved financial success. But I sense a restlessness in him that suggests if he could walk away, he would. My free-spirited younger son lives in a tent in 40 acres of wilderness in New Mexico. He is charmed by the remoteness and the grandeur of the vistas—and seems fulfilled, in a Scarlet O'Hara kind of way, to have found "his land." His challenge, of course, is economic viability. My thoughts move to my little grandson being baptized today. He is such a beautiful and expressive baby—he smiles with his eyes as well as his precious toothless grin. What gifts has he been given? How will he serve?

The service has progressed and the congregation is now renewing its own baptismal vows: vows that renew our commitment to determine our mission in life and find our reason for being in this world. A commitment directly related to the gifts we have been given and how we will use them in the service of others—our sending forth into the world as servants and stewards of the Holy Spirit. The ceremony concludes with the powerful and lovely prayer of baptism in The Book of Common Prayer: *"O Lord…Give us an inquiring and discerning heart, the courage to will and to persevere, a spirit to know and to love you, and the gift of joy and wonder in all our works. Amen."* Amen.

The Bucks County Herald, August 18, 2011

Remembrance

Iт's April, and my first robin of the season is perched on the deck railing outside my window. The sun is shining and the temperature is finally registering some warmth and thoughts of new beginnings.

Every April, in addition to turning to thoughts of spring, my mind and heart also turn to my mother's last days. The year was 1998 and Easter was April 12. She had invited a houseful of family and friends for a paschal feast, which she alone prepared. Since I lived six hours away, I wasn't present for the festivities, but spoke to her over the phone later that evening.

Her voice was a rush of delight and enjoyment, words tumbling over themselves to describe how nice it had been, what a good time was shared, and how much she enjoyed it all. It gladdened my heart and made me even a little hopeful, although the latest oncology report gave little reason for hope. She had beaten back the lymphoma for 10 years, but then slowly, insidiously, on little cat feet, it once again gained traction.

I had a visit planned for Mother's Day and was working on a family photo album as a gift for her. I knew she would love it. Sadly, she never got to see it. She passed quietly and peacefully less than two weeks after her Easter feast. My sister, stopping by for a visit after work, thought she was sleeping. She shook her shoulder, calling, "Ma?? Ma!" It took a while for the reality to sink in.

We were all stunned by the news. We knew her time was limited, but had been told months, maybe even a year. Instead, her last measure of life was meted out in days and hours. The chemo got to her even before the cancer did. None of us got to say a final "I love you" or "Goodbye." Worse yet, I worried I had never said "Thank you." Not then—maybe not ever.

Growing up, we didn't always see eye-to-eye, of course. Once I became a mother myself I saw things differently. Perhaps being a mother is a necessary step to gaining insight into the issues of our own mothering. There is nothing like direct experience to change one's perspective, to understand the trials of being a mother, to know how much one can love a child, and yet how challenging it can be to raise one. As we grow in this understanding, we can heal ourselves and contribute to the healing of relationships of all kinds. Our perspective not only changes—it enlarges.

It is easy to take one's mother for granted, to feel she will always be there, and to focus our attention on our need to separate from her, to blaze our own trails. However, "rather than separating from the mother...we are not, cannot be, separate from her," writes Clarissa Pinkola Estes, author of *Women Who Run with the Wolves*. "Our relationship [with our mothers] is meant to turn and turn, and to change and change...[The] mother is a school we are born into, a school we are students in, a school we are teachers at, all at the same time, and for the rest of our lives."

Now, much older and occasionally wiser, I find myself wanting to thank her all the time. My frequent thoughts of her most often take the form of appreciation and gratitude. I want to thank her for her support and advocacy, without which I would never have gone to college nor traveled across Europe as a student. I want to thank her for sharing her love of books and words, journeys and learning. Without her, I may never have acknowledged the existence of a higher being, the blessing of simplicity, or the magic of humor. Without her, I would not have known life itself. She was the school I was born into and, though she's gone, she remains the school in which I continue to… "turn and turn and change and change."

Thank you Mom—for then, for now, and for the rest of my life.

The Bucks County Herald, April 18, 2013

Treasure Hunt

It's that wonderful time of year for many things, not the least of which is a yearly trip with my sister from upstate New York. Younger than I by 10 years, she declared this annual event for the two of us a "must do" after our mom died. Given our age difference—and the amount of her care that was relegated to me as her oldest sibling—she views me as part sister and part mother. So Sis wanted to be sure we had some quality time together before one of us wasn't around anymore. (Probably me...) It was a great idea and we've shared some special times together in special places.

All our trips have been wonderful, but the one to "La Villa Real de la Santa Fe de San Francisco de Asis"—more simply known as Santa Fe—had some extra special aspects. It was a chance to visit with my younger son who lives in New Mexico, as well as enjoy time with my sister in one of my favorite cities.

We started—as we often do—with a spa day, then did the tram tour, stayed in a beautiful inn, had some fantastic dinners and, of course, shopped. But the very best part for all three of us was the unexpected adventure that arose out of my sister's desire to see if she could find any paintings by Jozef Bakos, the artist son of Polish immigrants who settled in Buffalo, New York—and who was also her husband's great uncle. Bakos left Buffalo in 1920 to paint in the clear light and magic of the Santa Fe high desert and now Sis wanted to try and track him down—or rather, track down his paintings.

To be honest, I was skeptical of the whole endeavor, despite her insistence that he was an important artist. We stopped in one gallery after another that had never heard of him. Then, just as I was about to drop out of the search, a kindly proprietress picked up a directory and aha!—found that a local fine art gallery did indeed carry Bakos paintings. The directory indicated the gallery was at the foot of Canyon Road. And so we were off!...by a couple of miles. Apparently the directory was outdated, and the gallery had recently moved to the *other* side of Santa Fe.

We trekked our way, still on foot, to the correct street but, unfortunately, turned west—not east—trudging along for several long blocks before realizing our error. My cynicism was now allayed, but my feet were screaming. We spotted a café and decided it was time for a respite. I pulled out my cell phone (why didn't I think of that earlier?) and reached Victoria Addison, owner of the gallery. She did indeed have four Bakos paintings and would love to have us visit, but was just on her way out. Could we stop by in the morning?

The next day, before starting out on our planned trip along the Turquoise Trail, my sister, my son, and I headed over to the gallery. Victoria was delightful, knowledgeable and gracious, despite still being in the throes of her recent move. Nothing had even been hung on the walls as yet. After a quick search, she found one of the paintings and put it on a free-standing easel. We stood and looked, silently turning our heads from one side to another like a trio of German Shepherds.

We weren't exactly bowled over by the work. But my sister asked the all-important question, "How much?" "Oh, that one's an oil from the 1930s—a very popular period for him. It should sell for about $24,000!" We all almost passed out. My sister laughingly admitted the family still had several Bakos paintings and the one she and her husband owned was down in the basement next to the furnace!

The gallery owner could barely hide her excitement—a previously unknown but potential treasure trove had just landed on her doorstep. Delicately, she indicated that if the family would ever like to sell any of the paintings, she was a willing buyer. My sister made the call to Buffalo; the return call came within the hour—all but one cousin agreed they would really like to sell!

This might seem like the end of the treasure hunt, but as it turns out, it was not.

The next day our little trio, once again on foot, wound its way through Santa Fe in search of the Georgia O'Keeffe Museum. We were still buzzing about our discovery when I noticed some bronze plaques embedded in the sidewalk and stopped to examine one. I was stunned to see that it was a tribute to none other than Jozef Bakos! Like the famous Stooges, we all piled up behind each other gawking at the sidewalk in amazement.

Then, looking up, we realized we were standing in front of the New Mexico Museum of Fine Art. All thoughts of O'Keeffe were set aside as we rushed in to this museum to see if they held any Bakos paintings. We were advised they did own Bakos paintings as part of their permanent collection, but none were currently being exhibited. Perhaps we'd like to check the gift shop for a poster or book on Bakos?

We would and we did, finding two great books that gave us more insights. Bakos was one of "Los Cinco Pintores," several of whom had studied together at the Albright-Knox Art Museum in Buffalo.

These five painters had a wild reputation as a result of their fun-loving party going, prohibition violations, and radical politics. In time, they each built an adobe hut off of Canyon Road. They became known as the "five nuts in mud huts."

We bought the books and returned to the hotel to read and learn more about this colorful group. We recited anecdotes to each other from our various sources, and marveled at how wild and free they all were. Then, in one of the books, we found the full name of the road where the huts were built. My son jumped on his computer to get directions. We grabbed our packs and jumped into the car, all giggly and excited to continue the hunt. And quite a hunt it was.

We first found the home of one of the other pintores, Will Shuster, who had painted his name on an exterior wall of his "hut." We stopped the car and piled out. The owner was gracious and confirmed its origins. She apologized that it was not a good time to show us through but offered the great news that Bakos' house was just up the road and easily identified by the For Sale sign out front.

We easily found the house, now greatly enhanced from its original humble beginnings. Not wanting to lose a special marketing opportunity, the For Sale sign noted that the home belonged to Jozef Bakos, one of the Cinco Pintores. The surrounding wall gate was locked so we called the realtor who, unfortunately, was miles away on his way to dinner with friends. He was helpful though, advising we could drive behind the house and access the yard to peek in the windows. We were delighted by all we saw. But before I hung up, my sister mouthed to me, "How much?" Would you believe $1.23 million?

At that, my son vowed the first thing he was going to do in the morning was buy a set of paints!*

The Bucks County Herald, May 16, 2013

*Two months after our adventure, my sister and her husband gathered several Bakos paintings in their home from willing-to-sell family members. Victoria flew to Buffalo to see them. Some were not oils, and some were not the primary period of interest, but she shipped all of them back to her gallery in Santa Fe, had them cleaned, and began showing them that summer. To date, all but one have been sold to collectors around the country and world. My sister's casual curiosity turned into true treasure for her family and helped alleviate some concerns over college tuition for her children. Just as important, it was also a fun-filled adventure for her, me, and my son—"Los Tres Investigatores," that provided a unique experience that we will all treasure forever. There are some things even money can't buy.

**Jozef G. Bakos, *Untitled*, 1935, oil on Masonite, 35 3/8 x 47 ½ in.
Collection of the New Mexico Museum of Art.
Gift of anonymous donor, 1984 (1984.578)**

"I'm Having a Baby Sistah!"

MY GRANDFATHER FAVORED BOYS. NOT that we granddaughters ever felt unloved or unwanted by any means. He just enjoyed the rough and tumble of boys. Boys who might want to be a coal miner as he had been. Boys who might want to go hunting up in the mountains with him and the hounds. As chauvinistic as that might sound today, it was pretty realistic for the times.

His three children granted four grandsons and six granddaughters, but his grandchildren—ah, we were a more compliant bunch, at least those of us who had children while he was still alive. Nine of the 10 of us grandchildren who bore children during his lifetime generated a perfect score: 14 out of 14 bouncing baby boys. In spite of the fact that three granddaughters were born after he died, somewhere in my psyche a seed had been planted—a seed that blossomed in spite of the drought on rational thought. This seed grew into the unconscious notion that babies born into our family would be boys.

My daughter-in-law, however, knew otherwise. Her body sent signals during her second pregnancy that were totally different from the first—the one that gifted us a beautiful baby boy. With full confidence in the pinging of her intuitive antennae, she videotaped our grandson making an important announcement—even before the ultrasound confirmed it.

Our not-quite-three-year-old reporter, in spite of several outtakes and an adorable speech pattern that occasionally emulated gangsta rap more than the King's English, finally conveyed the message: "I'm having a baby 'sistah'"! The communication was clear—a baby girl was on the way.

A girl! Oh my. I didn't expect that! In spite of having had a baby sister and being a girl myself, I just didn't expect that. I mean didn't we always have beautiful boys? It took a while—but not really all that long—for the idea to sink in. And once it did—I was jubilant! "It's a girl!" I trumpeted to any and all who would listen. "We're having a baby girl!!" I hadn't realized how thrilled I would feel at such news.

Our first overnight babysitting assignment with her was when she was 10 months old. We were assured that unlike her high-energy brother, she was a "Zen" baby…Not even close. Our little darling is an amazon—in the best possible meaning of the word. She's strong and confident, fearless and determined—and have I mentioned?—way too smart.

This is what amazes us. She's every inch a tiger, while also being every inch a little princess, loving her bows and ribbons, and ruffled nightgowns adorned with the obligatory images of Minnie Mouse and characters from *Frozen*. She wants to roll and tumble with the boys, and play beauty salon with me.

I think again of my grandfather, who was gentle and compassionate as well as fiery and fierce. A person of history, he worked with John L. Lewis and many others in the founding of the United Mine Workers, eventually rising to a role as district vice president. I see the same fierceness, determination, and leadership qualities in this "baby sistah," woven in amongst the ribbons and lace of her princess costumes.

She's definitely going to be a president someday. Whether it's of a company, a club, a college, or the country—we'll have to wait and find out. In the meantime, we have the joyful experience of a fierce and precious baby girl to love. My granddad would have heartily approved of this "sistah,"—his incorrigible and compassionate, opinionated and kind, great-granddaughter. After all, with the definite exception of the ruffles and ribbons, they are so very much alike.

August 2016

Grandparent Sitcom

I AM AN AVID NETFLIX fan and recently rented the movie *Parental Guidance* starring Bette Midler and Billy Crystal. It is a tale of outrageous events and cross-generational insights that arise when the grandparents babysit for a weekend. It's just the sort of goofy sophomoric one-and-a-half star film I would never deign to rent—until I became a grandparent myself. Now I'm living some of those outrageous scenarios.

One comedic situation started harmlessly enough. I had to stop by Staples and drop off a computer cable before delivering my two-year-old grandson to his home, followed by a ladies' lunch. Easy enough. It was a beautiful warm day and I selected a lovely eyelet top that required a strapless bandeau vs. traditional undergarment. My grandson and I walked into Staples holding hands. So far, so good. Then I released his hand—for just a second—to get the cable out of my tote. That's all it took. He was off, arms and legs windmilling as fast as they would go, running up and down the aisles squealing with delight. I dropped the cable, shouted my name over my shoulder to the technician, and took off after him. It's not the most decorous look on an older adult.

He loves to play hide and seek, and after unsuccessfully tracking him from behind, I finally ran ahead a few aisles to head him off at the pass. He was wriggling mightily as I scooped him up. By now, my bandeau was no longer doing its intended job; rather it was twisted around my waist, constricting my blood flow and leaving sensitive areas unsupported. Normally I would have been glad to drop his 33 pounds back on the floor, but there was no way I wanted to risk more hide and seek and—more importantly—I needed a modesty screen! We must have made quite a sight as he wriggled and I grappled all the way out of the store, through the parking lot, and finally to the car.

Another adventure ensued at the YMCA after swim lessons. Getting into the pool was relatively easy. Showering and dressing afterward were the challenge. He was happily seated, playing with the hand-held shower head, so I decided it was a good opportunity for me to dry off and get dressed. Mission accomplished. Now it was his turn. Just as I reached in to turn off the water he turned the shower head toward me and the spray hit me full force. I now looked like an also-ran entrant in a wet T-shirt contest. The walls of the dressing room didn't look much better. With the help of a hair dryer and strategic frontal placement of our tote bag full of swim paraphernalia, I figured I could make it through the lobby and out the door with a modicum of dignity and invisibility. That was before I realized he had—with one quick stealth move—reached the toilet paper roll and was dragging a trail of Charmin behind us all through the hall.

Grandpa had fun too when dressing him for an event. I choked down laughter as I saw the result of trying to wrestle an alligator into a nice outfit. His shirt was going in the right direction, but his dressy gray slacks were on backwards, pockets facing the wrong direction, and his shoes were on the wrong feet. Add to that the confused look on both their faces, and you have a sitcom-worthy scene.

Wisdom, on the other hand, requires a four-year-old. Our granddaughter wanted a peanut butter and marshmallow fluff sandwich for lunch. I explained I could offer only peanut butter with jelly. "Why?" she asked, aghast at such a shocking circumstance. I explained I didn't really like the taste—or even the idea—of marshmallow fluff. She considered this thoughtfully for a moment before responding with shrugged shoulders, "Well, maybe when you're older..."

Art Linkletter, the 1950s radio and TV host, continually aired vignettes demonstrating that kids say—and do—the darnedest things. With another grandson's recent birth and a new granddaughter's arrival early next year we are assured of a continuously full barrel of monkeys and many more seasons of our personal grandparent sitcom. And we wouldn't have it any other way. These little miracles bring joy, laughter, and learning into our daily lives and we are beyond grateful for their presence.*

The Bucks County Herald, September 19, 2013

I'm happy to say that as of this writing our barrel of monkeys now holds five brilliant, beautiful, and very funny grandchildren.

Veterans' Stories

IT WAS THE DAY AFTER Hurricane Sandy, and only I, and our intrepid leader, John, showed up for the scheduled town walk through the cemetery. The ground was littered with debris, the decorative iron fence marred by the force of a fallen tree. As we walked the paths, John began picking up the small American flags, now strewn about the landscape, honoring the veterans buried there. He returned the flags to their graveside medallions.

As I joined him, I was struck by the breadth of our indebtedness. The earliest inscriptions we found were for the Spanish American War (1898). There were many markers for GAR—Grand Army of the Republic—designating service in the American Civil War (1861-1865). Some tombstones and medallions for the first European war (1914-1918) just said World War, devoid of a number, and serving as a reminder that this war was to be the war "to end all wars." But, of course, it did not. Rows and rows of medallions, lined up like corn in an Iowa field, spoke to the apparently unending nature of war.

In quick succession we saw markers for those who served in World War II, Korea, Vietnam, the Persian Gulf, Iraq, and Afghanistan. Too many markers, too many wars, too many bodies.

If you stand quietly and close your eyes, you can almost hear the heartbeats. Their presence gives one pause.

As we continued to walk we noticed a monument for the Stryker family. We were specifically drawn to the headstone for Captain Frank P. Stryker: "Killed in Battle at the Elbe River, April 14, 1945. Buried in Margraten, Holland, R.I.P." We knew the Stryker name from our walks through Maplewood, the post-World War II neighborhood, where a grateful citizenry named the streets for Stryker and fellow comrades-in-arms: KREUTZ, MYERS, GLEN, MILLER, KERSHAW, CHUBB, WALTON, MCLAUGHLIN, MCCONNELL, and TAIFER. A Veterans Park and dedicated memorial site acknowledge "…the freedoms gained for us by those honored dead."

Our liturgy last year prompted me this year to embark on a pilgrimage of sorts to other memorials around town. The courthouse lawn at a central crossroads forcefully reminds us that "Freedom isn't Free." Thanks to a project undertaken by Gold Star families and the county commissioners, we not only read the names of those who served and died, we see their faces. I feel the stinging pinpricks of tears. Not just names, but faces. Names, faces, and ages—ranging from 19 to 43, most in their 20s. Their lives given in Pakistan, Iraq, and Afghanistan.

Our town is the county seat and memorials abound, including one of the first Civil War memorials in the country. This defining obelisk honors the 104th Regiment of Pennsylvania Volunteers Infantry as well as Colonel W. W. H. Davis, a prominent citizen and founder of the Bucks County (Pennsylvania) Historical Society. To raise the money for the monument, surviving members of the regiment baked bread and sold it to the Union Army. How novel—the military holding a bake sale to raise funds!

Davis established Camp Lacey on what is now Memorial Field at a local high school. His stern leadership forced weekly baths and smallpox inoculations which resulted in much grumbling among the men, but the reality of war and pestilence soon revealed Davis' wisdom. After their training, 1,049 men departed to become part of the Army of the Potomac. Regimental losses are listed on the plaque, again reminding us that armies are comprised of individuals, and that freedom isn't free.

World War II veterans are honored nearby, as are those who fought in Korea, the Persian Gulf, and Vietnam.* The graceful arc of the Vietnam memorial offers an important reminder as it also pays tribute "… to those…who did return, yet later died or suffered due to debilitating physical or emotional pain…"

Vietnam Memorial, Doylestown, Pennsylvania

Looking around, I notice a solitary pink rose adorning the base of a small pillar and move closer to investigate. It is a tribute to others who have died in service to their community: police, fire-fighters, and other law enforcers.

Walking down Printers Alley to Pine Street, I encounter the rich mosaics of Freedom Square, commemorating the leadership and "service above self" demonstrated by two young local residents, both killed in Iraq. This memorial not only honors the fallen, but also challenges the living, asking the provocative question, "Do we take liberty for granted?"

My journey then leads me to the County War Memorial sculpture at Broad and Main, dedicated to "...these memories of service and sacrifice" given in all wars "...in the defense of our country..."

Our beautiful community reminds us—in all its corners—of those who have given the ultimate sacrifice in preserving for us the ideals of liberty and justice and freedom upon which our nation is founded. It has been a rich and inspiring activity to move among these memorials and grave sites, acknowledging each one. It has left my heart heavy, but also grateful.

It is important that we remember.

The Bucks County Herald, November 14, 2013

*I dedicate this article to all veterans, but most especially to my brother, Donald Steinkirchner. He was a proud member of the navy and served in Vietnam. He returned home to a nation that unfairly judged those who served, rather than those who made the decisions to pursue such a conflict. Despite the hostility, he used his skills, intelligence, and work ethic to develop his trade, learned on an aircraft carrier. He successfully reentered society and has provided a secure home for himself and his family ever since. I am very proud of him.

Return of the Prodigal

He HAS ALWAYS BEEN AN exercise in detachment.

When a sophomore in high school, he and two Israeli class-mates spent the summer on a kibbutz located near the Lebanese border. And yes, there were border hostilities at that time.

At 17, he applied for a grant from the Student Conservation Association to participate in its sole international offering. He was advised to apply for a domestic program because the international program was the most competitive. He ignored the advice, wrote his essay—and was one of 12 Americans, nationally, to be selected to join 12 Soviet youth to work on conservation projects in Yellowstone National Park and a national park in Latvia (part of the Soviet Union at the time).

After graduating from high school—with special honors in mathematics—he eschewed college and set out on a life of adventure. He and a buddy signed on as crew for a private yacht. They thought it would be fun to cruise the Caribbean for several months. But the owner was a bully so they jumped ship in the Dominican Republic. Soon after, they landed in Australia working on a pig farm near Perth. The Aussies were kind to them and he really enjoyed the people, culture and beaches of Western Australia.

But the siren of San Francisco called, and so he responded. Using his carpentry, masonry, and sailing skills, he earned enough money to buy a 20-foot sailboat. He named it Orion and moored at Fisherman's Wharf, which offered locker room facilities to "residents." Orion became home. He likes high-rent locales and good food and drink. Otherwise he prefers to live minimally, in concert with nature and the tides. Even MacGyver, the resourceful TV action hero, would have applauded his inventiveness in achieving it all with a single stroke.

When rent at the marina took a big jump, he pulled up anchor and sailed across the bay to Sausalito. While there, he became interested in catamarans. He helped a friend build one and decided to trade in his single hull for a double. When a local ordinance limited the amount of time one could anchor in the harbor, he left Sausalito and, with two friends, sailed his catamaran to Catalina Island—in the perfect storm.

His teens and 20s came and went; so too his 30s. He eventually decided to leave the seafaring life and become a landlubber. A chance conversation on an airplane flight landed him in the deserts of southern New Mexico, serving as a foreman for a wealthy Texas financial advisor who was rehabilitating an old ranch. Life was good and we all felt he had found his niche. Then 2008 arrived with all its attendant financial mayhem. The financial advisor started to feel less wealthy and by 2009 the foreman was out of work.

An ad on Craigslist took him north to La Villa Real de la Santa Fe de San Francisco de Asís: Santa Fe. Holy Faith. He took odd jobs and somehow convinced a land seller to hold a mortgage on 40 acres with a minimal down payment and minimal monthly installments. He pitched an old army tent on his "land" and then faced the prospect of affording it. He found a position building yurts.

But the Great Recession and cold, harsh winters took their toll there as well. He struggled. His 30s waned and soon the big 4-0 came and went. He experienced obstacles and frustration as he tried to realize his dream of being a homesteader and living a self-sufficient, sustainable life.

"Becoming" is a serious and challenging business and every path is different. Some paths are more challenging than others. I glance at my bookcase and see the matryoshka dolls I brought back from a trip to Russia. They are all lined up. The smallest, then the next larger, and then the next and next, growing incrementally at each step. It's all a process, and it takes time, and sometimes it's glorious and sometimes it's just terribly messy. Santa Fe. Holy Faith. Let go and let God.

Many lovely ladies have come and gone in his life. He is sweet, tall and handsome, and charming. I'm sure many of those ladies love him still. But they passed on a future with him because of the insecurity of the nest. Last summer, a new woman joined him on his annual visit. She was lovely and very much in sync with his philosophies on life and nature. Her oldest sister was born in a teepee. She wasn't fazed by his rustic lifestyle.

Time passed and an announcement was made. They'd known each other less than a year. Fear clutched at my heart. Santa Fe. Holy Faith. Let go and let God. We made a visit and were reassured by their loving manner and commitment to each other. A new baby is a powerful manifestation of hope and faith. Holy Faith. As the little hand curled around his finger, the new father nuzzled his baby's sweet-smelling soft dark hair and kissed his fat little cheek.

He exchanged a look of love and pride with the lovely lady. In that moment the realization hit me—my prodigal son was home at last.

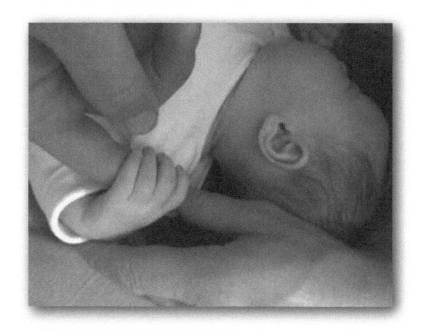

The Bucks County Herald, August 20, 2015

This article generated the greatest response of any that I have written. Many readers also had prodigal children, both sons and daughters. Some wrote to say they too were "prodigals." The piece has resonated for many people on many different levels.

Part Five:
Relationships

"Yet, taught by time, my heart has learned to glow
for other's good, and melt at other's woe."

HOMER

Valentine's Day

"I LOVE YOU MORE TODAY than yesterday," the little plaque sweetly began—and then quickly disposing of saccharine sentimentality, it twisted our expectations by ending—"because yesterday you really pissed me off." We simultaneously dissolved into laughter, totally relating to the sentiment.

For many people age 65 or so, the larger vicissitudes of marriage have long since been resolved, the sharp edges worn down, and a shared lifetime of experiences melded into a solid foundation built over 25, 30, 40 years and more. We, however, having married in 2006, when we were both 60 years young, are still relative newlyweds.

The Swiss psychoanalyst, Carl Jung, felt that relationships of all kinds were a key way that God speaks to us (as in "hello there—here's my gift to you and here's what you need to learn"). Jung believed that all relationships held the potential for transformation, but the greatest potential of all was offered by romantic love and marriage, for it is these relationships that offer the most intense "temenos" (the container into which alchemists placed base metals and then applied heat and pressure to transform them into gold).

Jung also theorized that, despite our egocentric belief that WE select our mates, our subconscious is really what is in control in picking our partners. How terrifying. No wonder romance and marriage can sometimes be a train wreck of colliding perspectives, preferences, values, goals, wounds, assumptions, et cetera, et cetera. Yet Jung believed that if we but approach our relationships with a sense of "agape" (loving hospitality), we could transcend our conflicts and move to a higher place of complementarity...wholeness... atonement (at-one-ment) that ultimately helps to plug the holes in the Swiss cheese of our psyches.

In the recent movie, *The Kids Are All Right*, Julianne Moore's character delivers an emotional scene in which she stands in the living room in front of her spouse and kids and passionately conveys the obvious: marriage is *hard*; relationships are *hard*. And despite all that, it's where she wants to stay. I am reminded of a Starbucks cup, pinned to my bulletin board, which quotes a New York City customer and activist named Anne Morris: "The irony of commitment is that it's deeply liberating—in work, in play, in love. The act frees you from the tyranny of your internal critic, from the fear that likes to dress itself up and parade around as rational hesitation. To commit is to remove your head as the barrier to your life."

Our first marriages ended in divorce and we both lived on our own for a long time—he for 10 years, I for 25. Needless to say, we've had our challenges. But as we approach our fifth anniversary later this year,* I reflect on our shared commitments and our common ground: arts and culture, travel, the company of family and good friends, anathema to debt, a similar sense of the silly... and love. Yes, we have struggled with integrating our lives at this later juncture and, as a result, we are both learning and growing in so many ways. Through love and commitment, we are gradually transforming, both individually and as a couple. The push-pull of our "opposites" is like a rock polisher, smoothing away our sharp edges, and broadening our lives and our humanity. Valentine's Day seems a perfect time to reflect upon and restate our commitments.

The Bucks County Herald, February 10, 2011

On July 2, 2016, we celebrated our 10th anniversary in Colorado, where we were married.

The Luncheonettes

THERE ARE FIVE OF US—A pentacle if you will. Very appropriate since we are all women. We meet every four to six weeks to break bread together and share a range of topics that runs the gamut from breaking news, to public or personal events, joys, sorrows, challenges, dreams— in no particular order and without an agenda. With the clink of silverware on crockery and the hum of other diners in the background, our conversations organically flow, like a stream around rocks.

Sometimes we visit different local restaurants and sometimes we bring a pot luck offering to one of our homes. It's *always* delicious, because we're sharing it together with love and laughter.

We all agree we should have a name for ourselves, but we've never come to a consensus on what that should be. I like to think of us as The Luncheonettes. It is such a privilege to be part of this group. They are all so smart and beautiful and funny and feisty and interesting. They are psychologists, community activists, spiritual leaders, matriarchs, volunteers, and most of all caring people and friends. Our topics range from the ridiculous to the sublime—and back again. I always leave with an idea, an insight, a new learning, or a really hearty laugh—usually, all of the above.

Have YOU ever heard of Queen Boudicca? Of course not— because she's the "Warrior Queen you never heard of"! And I never had. And here's the part that I find so amazing—after that conversation—Queen Boudicca shows up while reading the charming book, *The Guernsey Literary and Potato Peel Pie Society*. The author is describing a painting, "The Countess of Lambeth as Boadeicea (sic), lashing her horses..." See what I mean?? It's so interesting how a topic will manifest at one of our meals, and then show up again in an entirely unrelated context, now holding meaning as well as mystery. This group never fails to raise my antennae.

I realize how much these women feed emotional, social, and even spiritual aspects of my life. They are friends individually, but as a group they wield even more power and influence. Participating in these get-togethers is a huge gift. Another example is the time one member suggested we have a meal where we all pick a recipe to prepare from the book, *A Taste of Heaven: A Guide to Food and Drink Made by Monks and Nuns,* by Madeline Scherb. It is a combo travelogue/cookbook of US and European monasteries. I selected a shrimp appetizer that required the French liqueur Chartreuse. I learned not only that Chartreuse is considered to have curative powers, but also that it has a history of intrigue and mystery, as described on page 4 of the book:

> *"Take one ancient order of monks who are especially reclusive, add a secret liqueur recipe that is known to only two monks in the entire world, and throw in a high-tech computer system that allows the monks to control distillation in a near-by town without leaving the monastery, and voila!... The monks got their secret recipe...from a Frenchman in the seventeenth century, but it was confiscated during the French Revolution. The French bureaucrats couldn't decipher the recipe [which is made from 130 herbs]...and eventually gave it back."*

Our next gathering is coming up soon—I don't know what the conversation will hold—but I do know it will be good for body, mind, and soul. As every woman knows, girlfriends matter.

The laughter you hear echoing around town just might be ours. May it feed you as well!

The Bucks County Herald, July 21, 2011

The Luncheonettes
Left to right: Kate Adams, Sue Walsh, Sue Houston, Kay Rock, Inez Bing

The Icon Group

WE CALL OURSELVES THE ICON Group. Three couples united by a trip to Russia and Estonia in 2005. The men sing together—two basses and a tenor—in a local community choral group. This trip was one of the organization's periodic international singing tours. During a rehearsal near the end of the tour, we non-singing wives met for lunch at an outdoor cafe on the main cobblestoned square in Tallinn, Estonia, under the town hall clock tower.

Our group had come to this picturesque medieval capital to join 25,000 (yes, 25,000!) other singers in a festival of Estonian song and music celebrated every five years. Singing is a point of national pride in Estonia and a way in which the country maintained its identity in the face of its many foreign invaders over the centuries. A fascinating documentary, *The Singing Revolution*, tells the story of this unique and amazing festival.

During that lunch, in the cool shadow of the landmark tower, we learned that our individual wanderings around Old Town had produced a similar result: we had all bought beautiful Russian icons. In Russia, it is illegal to take icons out of the country as they are considered important orthodox religious artifacts as well as national treasures. Having just left St. Petersburg, we were amazed to walk down a Tallinn street, look into the open door of an antique shop and see hundreds of Russian icons lining the walls.

The eyes of one locked with mine and pulled me across the cobblestones into the shop. It was a beautiful rendering of the Madonna and Child. To this day, I feel as if that icon chose me, rather than the other way around. When the clerk was wrapping it up, I had a panicky thought.

"Are you sure I can "buy and carry" this back to the US? We couldn't in Russia." She slowly raised her eyes to mine and summed up centuries of warfare, strife, occupying forces, and transition with two sentences. "This is Estonia. We're Lutheran."

Recently, the Icon Group gathered for one of our semi-annual dinners which we rotate among our homes. Our hosts had recently had their icon of St. George evaluated by an expert. She validated the late-nineteenth-century vintage and pointed out details they had not previously noted—most especially the ironic touch of the icon within the icon. This struck us all as a great discovery and the vintage validation was reassuring. We had purchased our icons on love alone, with an abundance of ignorance, and wondered what an expert might say about the other two. One of our members has long surmised the Russian Cyrillic on the back of her icon actually says, "You've been fooled!"

We laugh a lot with this group. We joyfully reminisce, share good food and wine, talk of future travels, and enjoy stimulating music and conversation. And before it all, we join hands and express our thanksgiving for the chance of friendship we have shared, the depth and variety of experiences we have known together, and the hope that God will grant us continuing good health so that we may continue our gatherings for a long while. We recognize the fragility of life and celebrate the preciousness that friendship adds to the dimension and quality of the days we have. We squeeze hands and break the silence. We savor the bounty before us. We banter in the candlelight and we don't return home until after midnight. Another iconic evening comes to an end.

The Bucks County Herald, June 21, 2012

The Pull of a Pet

I'M NOT WHAT WOULD NORMALLY be called a "pet person." I've never really understood the cost/benefit for all the responsibility. I marveled that people took it on. When my husband and I began to date in 2003, he was the proud owner of a sweet mixed-breed SPCA rescue dog who lay at his feet by the fireside. I knew that if our relationship moved forward it would, by definition, be the three of us. Any other option was clearly non-negotiable. And so, when we married, I gained my second husband and first dog.

Puppy's a handsome fellow, not too big and not too small, with floppy beagle ears and characteristic white blaze on his nose. His head follows the regal shape of a Golden Retriever's, giving him  poses and a profile reminiscent of the Great Sphinx. His fur is tawny in color and oh-so-soft to the touch. He sheds way too much and scavenges food anywhere he can, especially in the kitchen when my husband and I are trying to prepare a meal. But he rarely barks and is a friend to one and all, especially people and other dogs (but not cats, or other critters that his hunter instincts might regard as prey). He is appreciative of his care and feeding—especially the feeding—and is all in all, a very mellow fellow. As you can tell, he won my heart.

As I write this, this sweetheart of a pooch has celebrated his 15th birthday. About five years ago, he had a cancerous tumor removed from his gum line—not an easy surgery to perform—but one which proved to be very successful. Puppy rebounded and was declared cancer-free. We rejoiced.

Then, about three years ago, a groomer noticed a hard knob on his left hind leg. The vet said it too needed to be surgically removed. When we picked him up, he not only had stitches on his back leg, but also a large sutured cut on his right side. The vet had found an additional growth that needed to be removed. This news was very scary. Puppy's big brown eyes looked sad, confused, and disoriented. It broke my heart and I found myself biting back tears as I rubbed his neck and back. I was by now deeply attached.

Last month we had another scare. Puppy's legs were giving out from under him and he seemed dizzy, disoriented and unstable. His head tilted at an odd angle. The vet diagnosed his symptoms as "Old Dog Vestibular Disease." In most cases, the cause is idiopathic, i.e., "unknown." It begins acutely and most often resolves itself within a couple weeks. In other cases, the cause is a brain tumor. The vet prescribed a battery of pharmaceuticals from antibiotics, to steroids, to motion-sickness pills, to pain killers. We started the meds and held our breath. We feared the worst. But, yet again, Puppy rebounded. We are grateful for this reprieve, even as we reluctantly acknowledge there may not be many reprieves left.

Recently, the syndicated cartoon feature, *Marmaduke*, showed the large and lovable dog trying to sit in the lap of a startled visitor. The hostess, carrying a tea tray, reassures her guest. "Sometimes he seems almost human, but he's very good at being a dog." I cut it out and have it pinned to the bulletin board in my office as validation of what everybody who's anybody already knows—pets are people too.

Not too many months later, winter set in. Normally Puppy loved to romp in the snow as we let him out before bedtime. But day by day he romped less and less, until one night he just lay down in the snow. My husband and I looked at one another with sadness. He was telling us it was time. We scheduled with the vet for the next day. His passing was very peaceful. It was Valentine's Day.*

The Bucks County Herald, November 15, 2012

After we retired, we had the time to drive cross-country for our annual visit to Colorado. This enabled us to bring the dog too. And did he love it! He loved the car ride, the different sights and smells at every stop, and he was as excited as his master with spending time in Colorado. He loved to go on hikes with my husband and stalk the many deer he would spy, his hunter's heart oblivious to the size differential. A portion of his cremains have been spread in Colorado. The remainder is home with us in Pennsylvania.

Home Alone

MY HUSBAND IS A LONG-DISTANCE hiker. Every couple of years he heads off to remote mountains in far-away lands to experience the exhilaration of their savage beauty and endure the rigors of the elements. This year he headed to Patagonia. For those who may be wondering, Patagonia traverses Chile and Argentina—way, way down toward the tip of South America where all that remains of terra firma is a collection of bits and pieces of land that look like what's left of a slab of peanut brittle that's been smacked against a granite countertop.

People asked if I planned to join him. He would have welcomed that, but such exploits hold no allure for me. I'm in awe of his adventurous spirit and all the hard work he puts into achieving his dreams, but honestly, I'm more inclined toward treks to a spa. Even when he teased me that if I didn't go, he would be paired with a roommate named Francesca, I was as unmovable as one of his mountains.

These global perambulations are a thrill for him and hold a side benefit for me. As the old saying goes, we married for life but not for lunch. Not that he hangs around much when he's here. He's a very busy guy. But still, there are perks most wives would savor in having a couple weeks home alone. I'm not talking about a

Macaulay Culkin sort of adventure or an opportunity for late night parties with pool boys. These possibilities hold no more allure for me than, well, a trek in Patagonia.

Having been single for 25 years between marriages, it's sometimes nice just to have time to oneself with no one else around, no one else to consider. It's an opportunity to tune out the rest of the world and tune in to myself; a time to recharge and regroup. It's a time to read until all hours and sleep late, a time to hog the whole bed. It's a time when toilet seats stay down and closet doors stay closed; when quinoa and Brussels sprouts can dominate the menu. It's a time when I can keep the thermostat at a comfortable (for me) winter temperature of 70 degrees, and continuously listen to KYW on the car radio.

And so, the first week passed, and it was good. It is a good and right and joyful thing for spouses to have some time alone for themselves occasionally.

At the beginning of the second week, it snowed. My husband usually shovels the driveway. I reached into the cupboard for a clean cup—they were all still in the dishwasher. My husband usually unloads the dishwasher. Being sprawled all over the bed is starting to feel lonely; I grab for his pillow. There are movies to watch in the evenings, but I can't motivate myself to do it. That's something we do together, snuggled under a blanket on the family room sofa.

During my second week alone, my focus shifts to all the many things my husband does and how they add quality to my life. I am clearly missing him and wonder if he is missing me. My iPhone dings. A message from South America: he is fine but the weather hasn't been great and his roommate is keeping him awake with coughs and snores. (Francesca snores?) He sounds a little lonely and I think he, too, may be missing me, even in the midst of his grand endeavor. And then, the doorbell rings and my thoughts are affirmed. There, leaning against the jam, is a long enticing box from Flowers.com—all the way from the fragmented pieces at the tip of South America.*

The Bucks County Herald, March 20, 2014

In 2016, my husband gave me the "space" to write this book by trekking the Haute Route in the French and Swiss Alps, so I could be home alone without distraction. It is much appreciated.

The Empty Chair

WE CALLED OURSELVES THE ICON Group because of each couple's purchase of one during our travels to St. Petersburg and Tallinn. The icons created an early bond. The husbands all sang in a choral group that frequently traveled abroad. In addition to Russia and Estonia, the six of us have traveled together to Bucharest, Romania; Budapest, Hungary; Ljubljana, Slovenia and most recently, Scotland—from Edinburgh to the Highlands to Glasgow.

One of our members was always culling and telling jokes. "What is worn under a kilt?" he would tease, eyes twinkling, awaiting his chance to deliver an anecdote. Or he would quote humorous phrases known as "paraprosdokians"—expressions which go against expectations, resulting in a humorous or satirical effect. One of his favorites was, "When I get humility, I will have no faults at all!"

A favored joke he told was of a group of hunters who went to a remote cabin in search of large game. They agreed to rotate the cooking duties. Whoever complained about the meals became the next cook. Unfortunately for the first fellow, his companions determined they would eat whatever was presented, no matter how bad. He finally decided extreme measures were called for, so for that evening's entrée, he went outside and gathered moose poop, which he fried up with onions and other seasonings. As the group slowly and silently ate their meal, one hunter finally acknowledged, "This tastes like moose poop." Realizing the implications of his critique, he quickly amended, "Good though!"

This punch line became part of our group's patois when even a slight criticism—about anything—would cause one or more of us to shout out, "Good though!" And we would all laugh over and over and over again. It became the ultimate inside joke.

In January, our exuberant friend and his wife went to Quito, Ecuador, to meet up with a Galapagos tour. He had carefully planned and organized this tour—it was to be the journey of a lifetime. Two other couples joined them. They strolled through the labyrinth streets of Quito, savoring the sights and sounds, the beautiful people, the exotic smells. One evening they all enjoyed a glass of Ecuadorian chardonnay—which he selected—at a rooftop restaurant overlooking the Plaza de San Francisco. Dinner at a local restaurant specializing in authentic cuisine followed, with extra passion provided by a lively discussion on what each person was doing spiritually to light up their life.

Before dawn the next morning, he woke his wife to say he was having trouble breathing. A doctor and canister of oxygen were summoned. The doctor diagnosed bronchitis. He was wrong. By the time the sun came up, one of our Icons was gone—suddenly and heartbreakingly—while in a foreign land. Our group had planned to gather for dinner after their return, to hear all about the adventure. And gather we did. Only this time, we faced a devastatingly and unexpectedly empty chair.

We all wanted and needed to gather again despite the turn of events. We all had our anxieties about how it would feel. But in the end, his bright spirit pervaded and surrounded us, as we and his widow shared stories and remembrances, and laughed and cried and felt grateful for all the times we had together. A new chapter will now emerge, as it always must.

Oliver Sacks, physician and author, wrote an op-ed piece for the February 19, 2015, edition of the *New York Times*, to share with readers his diagnosis of terminal cancer. In his eloquent essay, he noted, "When people die they cannot be replaced. They leave holes that cannot be filled..." We all felt the hole, or chair, that couldn't be filled. Sacks also noted,". . . I have been able to see my life as from a great altitude as a sort of landscape, and with a deepening sense of the connection of all its parts."

I envision our friend looking down on us, as if from a great altitude, while reflecting on the different parts of his life. One can hardly ignore his many successes: an emeritus professor of the Wharton School of the University of Pennsylvania, co-founder of a business, avid golfer, accomplished chef and wine collector, singer and actor, community and company board member, father, grandfather, and—most of all—husband, to a bright and beautiful second wife whom he loved and adored.

Despite all this, he was also forged by times of great suffering. His oldest son, Trey, died of a brain tumor while still a young man. Another son has been diagnosed with Parkinson's disease. He experienced the heartache of divorce after a long first marriage, endured business challenges, and knew personal frustrations. He'd eaten his share of moose poop in traversing his life's landscape. And yet, as he peruses it all, I imagine—scratch that—I *know*—the corners of his mouth are turned up, smile lines crinkling around his eyes, as he struggles not to laugh while delivering his final punch line loaded with gratitude and perspective:

"Good though!"

The Bucks County Herald, March 19, 2015

*This article is my eulogy for one of the members of our beloved Icon Group, Dr. E. Gerald Hurst. Please reference earlier essay, "The Icon Group," also in this section.

Photo courtesy of Oliver Flint, Bucks County Choral Society

Tomorrow, God Willing

MY KNUCKLES TURNED WHITE AS I gripped the steering wheel. I was seething. I had just finished hosting a baby shower for a young woman for whom there would be no more babies. I wanted this to be special.

I did everything I could to make it just right: the venue, the menu, the flowers and favors. But after many of the arrangements were made, a friend of the mom-to-be called and begged to be involved, so we agreed she would be in charge of finishing touches.

The big day arrived and one-by-one, guest after guest filled the lovely light-filled room. Everyone, that is, except the friend who was so desperate to help and be part of things. We phoned, emailed, and texted her to see if she was okay. No reply. The staff was pressing to serve the meal. We had to start without her. Then, without warning, and two hours late, she flew into the restaurant as dessert was being served, her hair still wet from a hasty shower.

She had forgotten.

After the shower, my husband and I were to attend an all-male a cappella choral concert. He went on ahead—I needed to wrap things up with the restaurant and then I drove around awhile to collect myself. The concert had already begun when I finally arrived. I sat by myself in the balcony so as not to disturb anyone.

As I was getting situated, the men began to sing a lovely lyrical piece entitled, "Tomorrow God Willing." I snapped to attention. It was as though the text of the piece was intended just for me: "We do the best we can. We do the very best we can, and tomorrow God willing, we get to wake up and try again."

Composed in 2007 by Elizabeth Alexander*, its inspiration came from an unusual source. Rather unconventionally, she chose a quote from a monologue of Garrison Keillor, the host of National Public Radio's *A Prairie Home Companion*. The warm resonance of the men's voices and the simple wisdom of the words floated up to me.

The repetition of the unassuming phrases swirled around in my head: "We do the best we can. We do the very best we can, and tomorrow God willing, we get to wake up and try again."

I took a deep breath. The composition was like a message from God, urging me toward understanding and forgiveness, reminding me to keep focused on the bigger picture, on what was really important. The forgetful friend was an addled young working mother with a heart bigger than her present capacity could handle.

She did the best she could. So did I. I wanted the event to be perfect. It wasn't. But the mom-to-be still felt honored and special. And that was the point—that's what was important.

As we approach this season of Advent, of Preparation, I find myself remembering this episode from last summer and the power this particular piece had for me. I reflect again on how easy it is to be disappointed or judgmental with others—and ourselves. Holiday seasons, paradoxically, are often as filled with stress as with joy, making it all too easy to lose sight of the bigger picture, of what's really important.

I think again about Alexander's lovely song, and Keillor's humble but powerful words and the gift they offer—a message of charity worth repeating and a message of redemption worth remembering: "We do the best we can. We do the very best we can…" And if our best—for whatever reason—isn't good enough? Then "… tomorrow, God willing, we get to wake up, and try again."

The Bucks County Herald, December 19, 2013

*Composer Elizabeth Alexander has granted Kay Rock permission to use her name, the name of her composition, and parts of the lyrics for publication in Over the Hill and Gaining Speed.

Part Six:
Special Days

"It's the special moments that give us a lifetime of memories."

AUTHOR UNKNOWN

Happy Birthday Charles Darwin

AH, FEBRUARY. THE SHORTEST OF months, and in a snowy winter, it can feel like the longest. To hurry it along, we celebrate a litany of special days. Often missing from this list is the birthday of Charles Darwin, the English naturalist, whose theories and scientific conclusions still roil our social and political landscape. Marc Moreau, a La Salle University philosophy professor and department chair, decided to set the record straight by writing an editorial homage to Darwin revolving around two provocative questions: "Why can't Darwin and Genesis both be true?" "Why has our culture fabricated an unnecessary dilemma and divide?"

Religion is important to me. So is science. I am aware of the harm and outright evil that have been done in the name of both. Marcus Borg, a professor of religion and culture at Oregon State University, and author of *Reading the Bible Again for the First Time*, makes some interesting points. He regards conflict about the Bible as "the single most divisive issue among Christians in North America today." And, "...because of the importance of Christianity in the culture of the United States, conflict about the Bible is also central to what have been called 'the culture wars.'" He feels these culture wars arise due to two different ways of reading the Bible:

a "literal-factual" way and a "historical-metaphorical" way. Borg encourages us to take the Bible seriously—but not literally.

The invention of the Gutenberg press, new translations of scripture from "sacred" languages to the vernacular, and the binding of the many scrolls of scripture into a single volume created a portable and democratic Bible, accessible to all, unleashing a variety of individual and institutional interpretations. This created both a blessing and a challenge. Every week I participate in a small Bible study group which challenges participants to read beyond the literal words and wrestle with meanings that confuse or invite relevant human truth as expressed through ancient myth and metaphor, parables and poetry. Our discussion can sometimes get pretty feisty. Democratization can be messy. We don't always agree, nor should we. However, in the push-pull of our dialogues, differences, and mutual respect, a new level of understanding emerges that expands our individual thoughts and invites a broader truth, applicable to our lives.

Why *can't* Darwin and Genesis both be true? Consistent with good biblical example, Moreau follows his question with a question: "...does the appearance of contradiction rest on careless reading?" He goes on to point out that "According to Genesis, God creates living beings by saying, 'Let the earth bring them forth.' But on the questions of whether they were brought forth by quick fabrication or slow evolution, Genesis is silent." Books of the Bible were written by different people, with different experiences, in different times. Genesis itself is a compilation of several traditions and offers us TWO creation stories: one the poetic priestly version of God creating all things in seven days and nights, the other the ancient myth of Adam and Eve.

Genesis' creation stories contemplate our "First Cause," i.e., original creation. By contrast, Darwin's book is all about secondary causes. It is about the mechanisms through which life, however it began, diversified into the species known to us today. As Darwin himself states, those mechanisms cannot work "without living creatures that already exist and strive to perpetuate themselves."

Darwin was not trying to trump the ancient eloquence of Genesis or dismiss its mythological truth. When a reviewer of *On the Origin of Species* suggested Darwin was on the verge of explaining the origin of life, Darwin replied angrily: "It is mere rubbish... The mystery of the beginning of all things is insoluble by us." He further refused to present his theory as a "Theory of Everything." Darwin considered his scientific discovery as a unifying theory of the life sciences, which help to explain the diversity of God's creation. How ironic that it has become so divisive.

Nonetheless, perhaps Darwin's discovery still can help us find unity in diversity. Moreau concludes that "we escape...false dilemma[s] by reading... [or listening or speaking]... more carefully and with charity... [for] charity hunts for the truth in what the other person is saying." How evolutionary!

The Bucks County Herald, February 16, 2012

Graduation Day

It's THAT SPECIAL RITE OF spring. Everywhere, graduations are blossoming across the educational landscape and proving to be more an actual harbinger of spring than the cool damp weather. In this particular year, our family is celebrating the graduations of my niece and nephew—a sister and her older brother—who will respectively attain their bachelor of science and master's degrees this month. My niece will now begin rotations as a physician's assistant and my nephew will pursue his fortunes in supply chain management in San Diego—far away from his Buffalo, New York, roots and family. They have worked hard and we are proud of their accomplishments and excited and encouraged for their futures. This is an exciting time of transition and new beginnings: a commencement as well as a conclusion, as every featured graduation speaker will attest.

I reminisce on my graduations. In high school, I missed the valedictory spot by one one-hundredth of a percent. As our 50th reunion was being organized, many old memories surfaced—it seems that many people remember that nail-biter finish! At the reunion itself, the actual valedictorian good-naturedly relished again his razor-thin margin of victory. In my salutatory address that concluded our ceremony, I was clearly focused on the future.

I remember looking forward to college, to leaving home, being in a different environment, pursuing my choice of study. I have always enjoyed the academic environment, but soon realized my learning would expand far beyond the classroom as I experienced new people, new ideas, new foods, new values, and new situations. It was interesting, scary, thrilling, and occasionally startling.

That future focus carried into my college graduation ceremony as well. With my diploma in one hand and a suitcase in the other, I went directly to New York City to fulfill a long-held dream of living and working in the Big Apple. I did not go home, I did not pass "Go," and I definitely did not collect $200. The plan was originally hatched with my best friend from elementary and high school. By the time the opportunity came, she was a married mother, but I forged ahead, joining college classmates who were a year ahead of me. The timing was right as they were seeking an additional roommate to help pay the Upper East Side rent.

Every time I look back on this time in the Big Apple, I give myself a mental pat on the back. It was every bit the adventure I had hoped for and more. What's the saying—"God takes care of children and the ignorant"? I pretty much qualified on both counts and was guided by a hand I felt but never saw. I didn't know what I didn't know, so I walked in to an employment agency and walked out with a position as an editorial assistant in the New York offices of a British publishing house. It was an opportunity that took me all over Manhattan to event openings, interviews with actors, movie openings, lapidaries, and luncheons with speakers like Walter Cronkite. It was, in short, the job of a lifetime for a young college grad.

After a couple years, I too became a married mother. But divorce and single parenthood soon made my thoughts return to career options—something that previously occurred more through happenstance than consideration. I decided to pursue my interest in business. To enhance my credentials I pursued an MBA at Temple University in Philadelphia. It is a two-year program—and with diligence and hard work, I finished in six! As I look back on those years, working full-time, raising kids, managing a household, I think I got through them in a trance of sorts. Being stubborn also helped. I like to finish what I've started.

The graduation ceremony was held on an unusually hot day in May, but my mom, siblings, good friends, and both adult sons were in attendance to cheer me on, programs folded into fans to beat away the heat. My sister, who never saw a party she didn't like, delivered big time. I couldn't have asked for a more memorable day.

I am grateful beyond belief that I made it. It truly was a new beginning. And every spring, when I see young graduates from all levels of the educational ladder, I feel the warm glow of remembrance and silently or aloud offer each and every graduate a resounding HUZZAH! May you have the best of adventures in this new beginning.

The Bucks County Herald, May 19, 2011

Author with longtime "bestie," Sally Lehde
Johnston, 50th High School Reunion

From President's Day to Presidents' Day

FEBRUARY IS A SHORT MONTH with many special observances, including Groundhog Day, Tu Bishvat (the New Year for trees—one of the four New Years in the Jewish calendar), Valentine's Day, and President's Day. In this year of 2015, February also holds observances for Mardi Gras, Ash Wednesday, and the Chinese New Year. My research also revealed that International Condom Day, not surprisingly a day intended to promote use of condoms, is an informal observance in conjunction with Valentine's Day. February is a busy month, possibly with the intent of helping us get through it faster.

But I digress. My focus—and umbrage—has to do with the federal holiday of President's Day. Note the location of the apostrophe. Many people—and I used to be among them—believe that it is actually Presidents' Day (apostrophe after the "s"), and think it honors both Washington and Lincoln. It does not.

When the Uniform Monday Holiday Act was passed by Congress in 1968—designed to increase the number of three-day weekends for federal employees—it moved the celebration of Washington's birthday from February 22 to the third Monday in February. Lincoln, whose birthday was February 12, was not part of this official recognition. A push to include acknowledgement of Lincoln as part of this federal holiday *failed*. In other words, he was consciously excluded.

It particularly rankles my sense of justice this year, as 2015 represents the 150th anniversary of a series of events that ultimately led to the end of the American Civil War. In early April 1865, Lee and his besieged Army of North Virginia abandoned Richmond and sought to regroup at Appomattox. General Grant, in hot pursuit, was able to outmaneuver Lee and arrive before him. A battle ensued, but the Confederate soldiers were completely surrounded, and Lee determined the fight was now hopeless. He surrendered his army on April 9, 1865.

Word of Lee's surrender soon spread throughout the Confederate states, and other southern generals also capitulated. Andrew Johnson, who ascended to the presidency after Lincoln's assassination—only a few days after Lee's surrender—declared the war over on May 9, 1865. Stand Watie, a Cherokee brigadier general for the Confederacy and the last and final holdout for the Confederate cause, surrendered his forces on June 23, 1865. The hostilities had ended and the United States of America was preserved. No small war; no small feat.

The states of Connecticut, Illinois, Missouri, New York, and New Jersey still recognize Lincoln on his actual birthday. Several others recognize him on other dates. Many other states, including Arizona, Colorado, Hawaii, Idaho, Maryland, Michigan, Minnesota, Nevada, North Dakota, Ohio, Oklahoma, Oregon, Pennsylvania, South Dakota, Tennessee, Texas, Vermont, Washington, and West Virginia, have set an example for the federal government by consolidating both birthdays into one celebration on the third Monday in February. In these states, the holiday is correctly displayed as Presidents' Day. But at the federal level, it officially remains President's Day. No wonder we're confused.

I am proud that Pennsylvania is among the states that have chosen to honor Lincoln as well as Washington. It seems especially fitting that our state, the home of the Battle of Gettysburg—often thought to be the turning point of the war for the Union—would be counted among those that recognize this great man. It also would be fitting for the federal government to celebrate both Washington, who was steadfast in his determination to create and lead a nation of the people, by the people, and for the people—AND Lincoln, who was equally steadfast in his commitment to preserve said nation. Yes, yes I "get it." Many of the missing states were part of the Confederacy. But 150 years have passed since the end of the Civil War. We all derive value in being "One nation, under God." One only needs to observe Europe's struggles to realize the practical, economic and policy benefits afforded by our United States.

Surely officially honoring Lincoln's legacy with a national holiday is warranted—even as a combined holiday. This would in no way diminish the deserved recognition of Washington, but could emphasize the seminal importance of both men to these United States. Mount Rushmore recognizes both. So should the Uniform Monday Holiday Act. Much was sacrificed and much was given—by both men—for all that was created and all that has endured.

The Bucks County Herald, February 19, 2015

Diamond Jubilee

LIKE MANY LITTLE GIRLS, OUR three-year-old granddaughter has a fascination with All Things Princess—from Cinderella to Snow White, to Ariel and Belle, from Jasmine to Tiana to Pocahontas. From books and movies, to stickers and tents, puzzles, and place-mats—it's "princess this and princess that." I don't remember being so enthralled with imaginary princesses when I was a young girl. Perhaps that's because I was captivated by a real one—Elizabeth Windsor, titled at birth as Her Royal Highness Princess Elizabeth of York. Elizabeth was my princess.

While traveling in Kenya in 1952, she received word that her father, King George VI, had died. The Princess was now a Queen, at age 25. Even before the defining moment, she behaved as the one whom she would become. Her public duties began at age 14, dur-ing World War II, when she did a radio broadcast to offer encour-agement to children who, like her, had been evacuated from their homes. On her 21st birthday, she delivered another broadcast stat-ing, "I declare before you all that my whole life, whether it be long or short, shall be devoted to your service and the service of our great imperial family to which we all belong."

The coronation ceremony did not occur until June 2, 1953. The delay provided time for national mourning—and time for

Unaltered Tuck Company (now defunct) Postcard
Image: ***On the Balcony of Buckingham Palace***
The Coronation of Her Majesty Queen
Elizabeth, June 2, 1953, Source: TuckDB
Used in accordance with Creative Commons License Deed

planning an event of pageantry, pomp, and royal proportions. Television, having been invented just in time, enabled me to watch it all, cross-legged on the living room rug in front of our Philco TV, images dancing on the tiny black and white screen surrounded by the enormous cabinet. I was enthralled. Oh, the jewels in her crown and around her neck—they were breathtaking, and so large as to be unbelievable. But even a naïve seven-year-old knew they were real. And oh, the history, going back and back and back and back to…where? when? I didn't really know.

Is it part of our national heritage to be fascinated with the British monarchy? Are all Americans destined to be star struck Anglophiles? My husband says no. But he's from Kansas. His royalty wore sparkly red shoes and hung out with men made of tin and straw. I'm an easterner, born in one of the original colonies.

Maybe it makes a difference. I myself find it hard to understand why Britain's royalty fascinates me so. I'm indifferent to Swedish, or Danish, or Russian, or even Dutch royalty. But Britain. Ah. Land of Richard the Lionheart, Henry V and Henry VIII, Elizabeth I and—as of 1952—Elizabeth II.

Her Majesty celebrated her Diamond Jubilee this year. Sixty years on the throne. Both Britain and the royal family have endured many trials during those 60 years. And both have prevailed. And many from around the globe joyously joined them in celebration. It has been an occasionally glorious, often bumpy ride, but shrewdly branded, and admirably adapted, albeit sometimes later rather than sooner. Elizabeth II has been every inch a monarch in her philosophy and decorum. Other family members, apparently feeling no such constraints, have been left to make the tabloid splashes.

Princess Elizabeth of York's childhood was cut short by an untimely death and the events of history. But she has proven to be an admirable leader whose influence is felt around the globe. To mark this anniversary, she once again pledged her dedication to her realms. "In this special year, as I dedicate myself anew to your service, I hope we will all be reminded of the power of togetherness and the convening strength of family, friendship, and good neighborliness...I look forward to the future with a clear head and warm heart."

Hail to the Queen. Long live the Queen.*

The Bucks County Herald, July 19, 2012

In 2016, Queen Elizabeth celebrated her 90th birthday, making her Britain's longest-reigning monarch.

Labor Day and the Spirit at Work

LABOR DAY APPROACHES. IT IS time for our summer idylls to come to a close and return to a more focused, accelerated way of life. I reflect on what Labor Day means to me. So often viewed as an end, I also consider it a harbinger of new beginnings.

I remember how excited I would get as a girl, even as much as I enjoyed summer, to know that a new school year was about to begin. I could just feel the anticipation and potential of it all in the gradually cooling air of September.

I reflect upon Labor Day's goal to honor and acknowledge the contributions of American workers to our social and economic well-being and I ponder the implication to me as a retiree. What will my contribution be now? Yet again, the spiritual implications of work, the relationship to vocation (paid or unpaid), and the importance of discernment emerge in my consciousness as I sit on the cusp of this "other" new year.

Several years ago I attended a conference for career counseling professionals. Richard Bolles, author of *What Color is Your Parachute?*, the perennial best-seller on career management, spoke on how he studied to be a chemical engineer, but upon his graduation from college decided he'd really rather be an Episcopal priest. He had the entire audience laughing in sympathy as he described his parents' stunned dismay over his forfeiture of a presumed lucrative career (and all their tuition money) for a life of presumed poverty.

But, of course, that's not what happened. He did become a priest and after serving in New Jersey for several years was invited to join the staff at Grace Episcopal Cathedral in San Francisco. After moving himself and his family across the country, he was still settling in when budget cuts eliminated his position. But even in the fog of anxiety and anger, he realized many of his peers and parishioners were in the same situation.

An inveterate problem solver, he soon reinvented himself as an investigative reporter, determined to identify and understand the practical skills needed to be effective in the labor market. Ultimately, he self-published his findings into *Parachute,* which is still regarded by many as the "bible" of career management.

Bolles, in both his life and his work, received material and spiritual rewards by heeding his callings. (Notice we may have more than one.) But heeding a calling can be a scary business. It can involve making difficult choices, including disappointing or even alienating those we love. It may mean separating from some things we hold dear in the present, for the hope of a future manifestation.

The word "vocation" is from the Latin *vocare,* meaning "to call." A vocation is not about a job or a title or a paycheck. It is about our mission in life, our reason for being in this world. It is directly related to the gifts we have been given and how we will use them in the service of others. The message is clear—we have work to do.

And that work takes courage and endurance to make it happen. A calling often lacks specificity—adding to the challenge— often a lifelong challenge—to bring it to fruition. And even then, there are no guarantees. Discernment is hard work.

I consider this new opportunity of retirement and what it may hold.* I strain to hear a calling and am greeted only with silence. Perhaps I should just take a hike—and trust in the slow work of discernment, allowing ideas to unfold in their own good time, in the gradually cooling air of September.

The Bucks County Herald, September 1, 2011

*The vocation that emerged for me in retirement was the opportunity to pursue a lifelong dream of being a writer. I approached the Bucks County Herald *with the idea of a lifestyle column, "Becoming 65," that would cover a variety of observations and reflections in this new stage of life. I wrote my column for five years and then left that role to compile all those articles into this book,* Over the Hill and Gaining Speed. *Our callings can evolve!*

To My Grandson* on the Occasion of his First Birthday

DEAR CHILD, THERE ARE SO many things I want to share with you. So many things I want to say. But as a writer, I'll start with a letter: a letter about aspects of life that I consider Important. I am from a different time and of a different gender. By the time you are old enough to read this, I may be long gone and you may find my thoughts quaint, or silly, or even objectionable. But I hope not. At a minimum, I hope you will give my thoughts some consideration.

ON RELIGION: One of the gifts my parents gave me was the gift of faith. They each held that there was a higher power than our own and that worshipping in community was important. Participating in a church community has been an important source of strength, support, challenge, beauty, struggle, and joy for me through the years. Of course, many evils have been done—and continue to be done—in the name of religion. I would suggest that these evils are really in the name of dogma, or literalism, or even politics. They rob us of the ability to think for ourselves, have doubts, ask questions—and still be welcome at the table, regardless of where we are on the "belief" continuum.

My parents—your great-grandparents—were of different faiths. My father was Catholic and my mother was Protestant

(Methodist). I still feel sadness that we did not worship together as a family. Perhaps in an effort to meld the two approaches, I became an Episcopalian. What this relatively mild religious diversity did provide, however, was an understanding that there is no "one religion" that has a lock on our pursuit of a relationship with God. All enduring roads get us there—just by different paths. My prayer is that you will explore a variety of religious options and eventually pick one that fulfills you, supports you, provides you strength, grace and love, and—very importantly—also invites your questions as you move and grow along your path.

ON THE BIBLE: No discussion of religion would be complete without a few words about the Bible, a book too often used to justify and condone much behavior that can only be labeled as un-Christian. These disconnects are often due to literal interpretations that offer little recognition or understanding of the poetic and metaphorical nature of the Bible's language. A poetic language that has enabled continued relevance to Biblical wisdom through the ages.

It is important to understand that "Bible" derives from "biblia," which means *library*. Originally a collection of individual scrolls from different times and different perspectives, it is now bound and presented as one book. No wonder it seems confusing and contradictory! The Bible offers many viewpoints: the literal, the historical, the mythological, the metaphorical, and the psychological. For me, the last three perspectives offer the greatest relevance and insights. I personally see the Bible, especially Genesis and the Gospels, as an amazing treatise on the development of the human psyche.

If you pursue biblical literacy, I would encourage you to do it in a group, so as to hear a variety of perspectives, even as you form your own. This type of study has made all the difference for me in making scripture relevant to my life. Even if you have no interest in religion, the Bible is the inspiration, model for, and subject of, more art, thought, literature, music, architecture, and drama than most of us who live within its influence will ever fully know. To know about the Bible is to receive insight into much of the world's past and present culture and history. As a record of humanity's effort to find and know God and learn how to live in harmony with divine law, it is an important way to be informed as well as transformed.

ON EDUCATION: Another of my strong beliefs is in the value of education, both formal and informal. My own life experience confirms that many of life's greatest lessons occur outside the classroom—which doesn't render them any less important and valuable. These lessons are to be embraced and learned as soon and as quickly as possible. I also believe in the importance of formal education, both practical and theoretical. It provides us a general foundation that levels the playing field with cultural and social peers and helps us to understand and navigate the world around us.

Perhaps even more importantly, the completion of degrees and certifications also demonstrates an ability to solve problems, meet challenges, develop our areas of non-preference, cope with difficulty, and develop discipline. It is my sincere hope and desire that you will explore and endure and triumph in both realms of education, in whatever fields of study call to you.

ON TRAVEL: Travel is an exciting, expanding, energizing, exhausting, challenging and surprising endeavor. It is an amazing example of the value of "informal" education. It is also a means to experience the incredible diversity and fascination of this big world we live in. I hope that you will have the privilege and honor to travel far and wide, meet many people, and have many adventures—even as you continue to come home after each one.

ON THE ARTS: <u>Literature.</u> The poet Emily Dickinson wrote, "There is no frigate like a book to take us lands away, nor any coursers like a page of prancing poetry." That line has stuck in my head since high school, and how many times I have experienced its wisdom as I have devoured books of all sorts, fiction and nonfiction, poetry and prose. Books have taken me even farther than my physical travels; have opened up new worlds and insights; introduced me to complicated, fascinating people; and have been a companion, a solace, an inspiration, an anti-depressant, and a continual source of pure pleasure for me. I hope that you, too, embrace the joy of reading, and that it may serve as a source of education and inspiration as well as diversion for you.

<u>Music.</u> Much research has demonstrated the developmental benefits of learning to play an instrument or to sing. Whether you embrace music as a practitioner or an appreciator of others' efforts, it can provide soaring beauty, comforting traditions, and the opportunity to drive your parents and grandparents absolutely crazy with the popular music of your day, whatever that may be. I'm glad to see you already rocking and rolling to "the beat" of your musical toys and secretly hope that you'll continue to enjoy dancing. It would be a thrill for me to get out on the dance floor and "cut a rug" with my beautiful grandson!

<u>The Visual and Dramatic Arts.</u> Like literature and music, these arts—whether paintings, movies, opera, ballet, or theater—can speak to us in special ways as no other type of communication can. I know you will have the benefit of being exposed to a wide variety of all the arts. I hope that you will experience and appreciate as much of this treasure as you are able—even if it's not all to your taste at the moment—and recognize it for the richness it provides to life.

ON SPORTS: Even at such an early age, you demonstrate the strength and coordination of an athlete. I myself have no particular athletic abilities, but even so, I enjoyed intramural sports in high school, and sandlot baseball at home. Today I enjoy watching a variety of sports, but my special favorite is baseball (Go Phillies!). Sports can play an important role in personal development by pushing us to challenge ourselves, work as a team, and deal with disappointment in life, ourselves, and others—even as we strive for victory.

I look forward to seeing you explore the various options that will surely be open to you, and to cheering you on in whatever sports ignite your passions and serve your talent. Another practical side of sports is the real potential for full or partial scholarships to college. Sports are not just games. They are important developmental tools that can continue to serve you, long after the last play.

ON MONEY: I like it! But it's not everything. If you think of money as energy, it can help to prioritize how you get it and how you use it. I have lived both over my means and under my means, and it has always been more emotionally and psychologically comfortable when I've been able to live under my means. Sometimes that's not possible and we use the powerful tool of leverage (i.e., credit) to achieve our goals. But it can be a slippery slope and needs to be closely managed or it will turn into an avalanche that can bury us in a New York minute. Try to reserve use of leverage for your really important priorities that have long-term benefits, such as buying a home or getting a formal education.

ON SERVICE: We all have unique gifts. One of the key missions of our lives is to identify those gifts and how we will use them in the service of others, in ways grand or small. Like individual patches in a quilt, our different patterns add interest, beauty, and completion to the whole. Let your light shine!

ON FRIENDS AND FAMILY: I have saved the most important until last. Friends and family form the fabric of our lives. As wounded and imperfect as we all are, our relationships weave important threads of history and experience, challenge and support, love and sacrifice that form the tapestries of our lives. May your net be tightly woven and may you always know how special you are. I will love you forever!

The Bucks County Herald, March 15, 2012

Since I wrote this we have been blessed with several more grandchildren and now share a total of five. My wish for each one of them is the same as I have expressed here for my first grandson.

Part Seven:
Extraordinary Ordinary People

"Lighthouses don't go running all over an island looking
for boats to save; they just stand there shining."

ANNIE LAMOTT

I Hyke

AH, A NEW YEAR—AS FRESH and crisp and filled with potential as a blank sheet of paper. And yet—at least for me—the same old, same old resolutions: eat less, exercise more. The Internet regales me with blogs and articles to help motivate and inspire these goals, with entries such as "Exercises to Rev Your Metabolism," "Six Bad Excuses for Being a Couch Potato," and "20 Tips and Tricks to Make Exercise a Lasting Habit." As helpful as these articles might be, none of them has the power and influence over me as has an octogenarian mother of four, grandmother of 14, and great-grandmother of 11: Mary Ann Nissley.

When she was just a girl of 50, Mary Ann came across the book, *Hiking the Appalachian Trail,* published by Rodale Press. This lit the flame of her hiker's passion and ultimately led to a vanity license tag that proclaims "I HYKE." (The traditional spelling had already been selected.) Since that reading, Mary Ann has hiked the full 2,168-mile Appalachian Trail from Georgia to Maine, twice—once as a "through hiker"—and once using the

"sectionals" approach. Additionally she has hiked the 348-mile Long Path from New Jersey to New York, the Finger Lakes Trail in New York State, and many others across the United States, Canada, and the Alps of Europe. She does this while carrying a 45-pound pack on her back containing a tent, sleeping pad, and sleeping bag. She also likes to have hot tea and soup on the trail so the pack includes a small Coleman stove.

Initially, she would hike up to 25 miles per day, but now her daily treks are more in the 10- to 12- mile range. One time she hiked in the rain for seven days straight. She would take off her wet clothes at night, but had to put them back on again in the morning to continue her journey. When her grandchildren and great-grandchildren become old enough, usually 10 years of age, she tries to bring them along, two at a time. But mostly she hikes alone—raising some consternation from her family.

One morning she arrived at our weekly walking group departure point with her car totally embroidered with muddy bear paw markings. We fellow walkers were agog at her tales of wildlife encounters and all laughed in delight at her story of the bear who approached her while she slept in a lean-to along a trail. Summoning all five feet of her height and raising the hood of her sleeping bag above her head with outstretched arms, she roared fiercely and then, feigning a shotgun, POW! POW! scared him away. The trick, apparently, is to make the bear think you are bigger than he is and if that doesn't work, pretend to shoot him.

Another time when she was hiking the Mid State Trail in Pennsylvania, she endured two falls; the first fall injured a tendon. Then she slipped on a rock, hit her head and began sliding down the side of the mountain. She stopped her slide by grabbing onto a tree. Fortunately her children had insisted she start carrying a cell phone should she ever need to call 911. Six hours, 14 stitches, and a helicopter ride later, she asked her rescuers to put her back on the trail. "No!" was their emphatic response. So she slept in her car and drove home the next morning.

Her gait is characterized by a slight roll to the left, courtesy of a knee injury she sustained on the Katy Trail in Oklahoma during a spate of tornadoes. Rangers shook her tent at night, saying she needed to get indoors. A church basement, sheep farm, B&B, and diner offered shelter. However, she wasn't going to let anything as mundane as the weather keep her from her trek, so during the days, she continued on until one strong gust torqued her body while her feet stayed put. More than a little determined to finish what she started, she used her trekking poles for support to finish the trail. She had the laparoscopic surgery on her knee after she got home. She claims it doesn't hurt and she bikes six miles or more a day as her ongoing physical therapy.

Biking and walking are done after she completes her morning chores around the large three-acre familial home, which she maintains herself since her husband passed away in 2000. She confides she may soon be getting to an age where she'll need to hire someone to climb the ladder and clear out the gutters. "I'm already at that age," I confess.

She's had many close encounters while rambling about in nature, but also recounts many kindnesses—from shared food with fellow trekkers to the occasional soft bed, warm meal, and shower from knowing neighbors living near a trail. When people comment on her courage she brushes it aside. "I don't think of myself as brave," she contends. "I'm just a long distance hiker."

One of the highlights of Mary Ann's trekking career occurred during a recent August when 22 members of her extended family joined her on a hike up Pinnacle Peak, a high point on the Appalachian Trail in Berks County, Pennsylvania, to celebrate her

80th birthday. It was a mere nine miles: four-and-a-half straight up and four-and-a-half straight down. The temperature was a balmy 95 degrees. Mary Ann can't keep the smile off her face as she talks about it. "It's the most wonderful birthday gift I've had in 80 years," she exclaims. She was very proud and touched that her children—self-proclaimed couch potatoes—and her grand- and great-grandchildren, who ranged in age from six to 36, "...could and would do it for me."

The hike was a common achievement for Mary Ann, but for her family it was a gift of the highest order to eschew the obvious—which would involve an expensive restaurant and air-conditioning—to join her in her passion. Clearly still moved by their love and generosity, she breathes a sigh that conveys the depth of her appreciation. "It was just so exciting and amazing to me."

"So what's next?" I ask. Our indefatigable trekker never hesitates: "I had so much fun on my 80th birthday that I'd like to do the same thing for my 90th !" But, of course, there will be many more treks between now and then. Her excitement is palpable as she talks about her future plans. "This June, I intend to finish the final section of the Mountains-to-Sea Trail in North Carolina."*

Now that's inspiring.

The Bucks County Herald, January 16, 2014

Circumstances have delayed Mary Ann's original goal of completing this trail by June. She has, however, completed all but the easternmost leg. This section will take her to the Atlantic Ocean. She hopes to be joined by two of her great-grandsons when she completes the trail later in 2016.

The Storyteller

"CREATIVITY IS NOT JUST ABOUT painting a picture or writing words on a page," opines storyteller and author Ray Gray. "It's about creating a new life outside of the world one currently knows." To illustrate his point, he tells of his parents leaving the home they knew among coal and clay miners and moving to a mill town in western Pennsylvania. Working hard, they managed to save enough money to buy four acres of land. First they built a basement where the family of five initially lived. Eventually they were able to add a first floor, and then a second, each "roof-raising" offering a new perspective on his world.

Other examples of family patience and perseverance were modeled. His father had tried three times to hitchhike to California. Three times he failed, and with a family to support, he moved that dream to a "back burner" and spent 40 years in the steel mills of western Pennsylvania as a machinist. However, after retiring, he bought himself a Stetson hat and moved to Arizona, finally becoming the cowboy he always wanted to be. Early failure didn't daunt him nor diminish his dreams. His youngest child paid heed.

Initially, school was a challenge for Ray. A learning disability made reading comprehension difficult. He eventually learned to compensate for his dyslexia, but even so, his high school counselors discouraged him from attending college. They clearly didn't know about his role models. Disappointment and struggle did not define or defeat the Gray family. Ray applied and was accepted at a small college in Ohio.

During Ray's sophomore year, President John F. Kennedy uttered his famous call to action, challenging citizens to ask what they could do for their country. Ray's social activism was stirred and in 1962 he left college to join the Peace Corps. Leveraging skills gained in building the family home, Ray helped build schools in the Dominican Republic. This experience opened him up to new understandings and was a key epiphany in his personal development.

On his return to the US, he enrolled in Temple University's anthropology program. While getting his degree, social activism continued to drive his passions, and he started a center for at-risk youth in the local Hispanic community. After obtaining his bachelor's degree, he decided to attend Princeton Theological Seminary for a master of divinity. His goal was to return to Latin America and work for the church.

While at Temple, he married a young woman from back home. In due course, a son was born and another epiphany occurred. He and his wife had complementary work schedules which provided Ray the gift of abundant one-on-one time with his boy. Ray cared for him and played with him, soaking up each stage of development. Ray began to create stories for his son: all kinds of stories, from fairy tales to stories about the natural world, and real or imaginary people. A new calling, storytelling, beckoned, and he chose not to pursue ordination after graduation. However, with another child on the way, he also needed to earn money and so took a job in the steel mills in Fairless Hills, Pennsylvania, following a path his father had pursued years before.

For some it may have been a soul-deadening choice, but for Ray Gray it was creative problem-solving. The mill enabled him to provide financially for his growing family, and shift work allowed enough free time and flexibility to pursue his idea of writing stories for children and performing them in schools. Working in the mills also provided greater insight into his father's and uncles' lives.

It was a bold step to leave the security and steady income of the steel mill, but in 1974 the creative part of his nature prevailed. He bought a map and marked each school location. He met with every principal to explain why storytelling was needed. He became an evangelist—informed by his own experience—for children with different ways of learning. Over the following 34 years, he told stories to over a million school children.

Yet again, life took a turn. Divorced and single, he moved to Doylestown, Pennsylvania, in 1996. After several years, he met a new love and remarried. The storytelling business was waning and he was restless for a new direction. With his new wife's full support, they switched traditional roles. She continued her career in academe and he ran the home. One day, he picked up his well-worn and oft-read copy of Carl Jung's memoir, *Memories, Dreams, Reflections*. This book was like his bible. It gave him permission to recognize his true nature and provided a model for how to live with anxiety and ambiguity while working out his life's journey.

Gradually a new path coalesced. Ray shifted from storytelling for children to writing and dramatizing works for adults based on the ideas of Carl Jung. He has performed in England, Canada, and around the US for the past seven years. Ray is not restricting himself or his muses as he pursues new paths. He's thinking a lot about love and creating stories that explore love in all the ways that have been meaningful to him. He tells of being with his mother when she died. For six hours he watched her breathing stop—and start again. At the end, a tear slipped from her eye and down her cheek. It was a numinous moment. Caring for his mother for the last four years of her life is one of the "love stories" he is exploring. How will these memories be shaped and told? That will be another story.*

The Bucks County Herald, July 17, 2014

*Ray has written a memoir told through the lens of stories he has created over the past 50 years. The memoir is entitled GRANDPA JUNG'S LESSONS...for a slow reader. *It is available as a Kindle eBook at* www.amazon.com.

One of the Lost Children

Operation Pedro Pan was an airlift from 1960 to 1962 that brought 14,048 Cuban minors to the United States. Through the auspices of the Catholic Church, parents arranged their children's deportation to protect them from communist indoctrination, diminished opportunity, and a perceived threat from the new communist government. For these reasons and more, they sent them to America.

Her father was a lawyer, her mother a homemaker. They lived in a middle-class condo in Havana near the university. From the window, you could smell the ocean and see the palm trees swaying in the breeze. The steps to the university were broad and white and reminded her of photos of the Parthenon. Her dream was to one day ascend those steps as a student. The fates had other plans.

Life under the dictator Batista was harsh and full of inequalities, so at first her family welcomed Fidel Castro and his revolution. As his comrades came down from the mountains, bearded and wearing fatigues, her mother would prepare meals for them. But soon, the fabric of life began to change. The new regime nationalized housing and education, changed the currency, and issued ration books. Personal possessions and money were seized and people were being taken away.

Life was getting worse, not better. The situation was tense and although only a child, she could sense danger in the air. The failure of the 1961 Bay of Pigs invasion led to a bold decision. Her father fled to Venezuela to start a new life and law practice. Once established, he would send for the family. She later learned he had a price on his head.

Photograph courtesy of Cristina Sullivan
Image: Cristina as a child, with her father

A protected only child, she rarely went anywhere without a chaperone. But she was a teenager and when a friend urged her to come out into the ocean on a small boat to celebrate one of the "liberators," she went. Her relatives were frantic. When she finally returned home late that night and told of her adventure, her mother's ambivalence hardened into resolve.

And so it was on June 30, 1962, three weeks before her 16th birthday—the cut-off age for Operation Pedro Pan—her mother, aunt, and cousin took her to the airport. "It will be only for a year," they said. "You will learn English," they said. Agents put her into a glass-enclosed room. She could see her family, and they her, but they could no longer touch or hear one another. The far door slid open, and with one last look of teary farewell, she walked out onto the tarmac and into the plane. She would never see Cuba again. Cristina Lecuona Menendez became one of The Lost Children.

After she landed in Miami, Catholic Social Services initially placed her in a girls' camp, formerly an army barracks, and later with foster homes in Illinois. She cried herself to sleep at night overwhelmed by homesickness. Despite her sadness and the language barrier, she excelled at school. Her family valued education, had a strong work ethic, and stressed personal responsibility. So she went with the flow, learned English and her lessons well, and was accepted into college. She graduated in 1967 with a liberal arts degree. While in college she met Jim Sullivan and in 1968 they married.

Throughout those early years, her mother would call her and send family photos. She is grateful to have these mementos of her early life. She regrets not keeping her father's letters. Venezuela did not offer the new life he had hoped and his missives were often sad and depressing. At some point the letters stopped and his family assumed him dead, not knowing how or why.

Photograph courtesy of Cristina Sullivan
Image: Cristina with her godparents

A visa for her mother to leave Cuba was finally obtained in 1972. She went to Puerto Rico to join family members living there. Eventually Cristina brought her to live in Bucks County, Pennsylvania. But 10 years had passed. Her daughter was now "Christine Sullivan," a married woman with a son. A daughter would soon follow. Cristina had integrated into the American culture and mores. Her mother could not. She missed her sister, café cubano, a tropical climate, and the Spanish way of life. A gulf larger than the distance from Cuba to Key West developed between them, and soon her mother returned to Puerto Rico to live out the remainder of her 98 years.

After college, Cristina came full circle and became a social worker for Catholic Social Services. After her children were born, she loved being an at-home mom. But her family had instilled her with a strong sense of social responsibility and when the children went to school, she helped open the Bucks County Health Department clinic in Doylestown, Pennsylvania, and later worked in a nursing home. Ultimately she went back to school for her teaching certification and taught Spanish in the Council Rock school system for 18 years, retiring last June—nearly 50 years after arriving in this country.

Even in retirement, she is still very much her parents' daughter. Cristina volunteers for the Michener Art Museum, Doylestown Hospital, the American Association of University Women, and will soon serve as a translator for the Ann Silverman Health Clinic. She recognizes that time and again, opportunities found her and she is beyond grateful for the life she has. She cannot imagine living in Castro's Cuba.

But every now and then, she looks out her window and wonders, "Where are the ocean and the palm trees?"*

The Bucks County Herald, September 18, 2014

Since this article was published, Cristina has been approached to serve as a consultant for a play about Operation Pedro Pan that is being produced for the Arden Theater in Philadelphia, Pennsylvania.

Additionally, since this article was written, the United States and Cuba are moving forward after more than 50 years, to normalize relations between the two countries. Cristina would love to take her children to visit Cuba, but is reluctant to do so while the Castro regime remains in power. She is watching events closely as they unfold.

Life Goes On

It started as a weak feeling in his legs while helping care for three young grandchildren in North Carolina. He had awakened the kids and gone downstairs to start breakfast and prepare school lunches. As the weakness overcame him, he sat down. When he tried to stand, he couldn't. His son-in-law drove him to a local healthcare facility where the diagnosis suggested a rare autoimmune disease.

It wasn't until he was transferred to a large regional hospital that an MRI determined the blood supply to his spinal column was blocked by a clot. He had had a stroke and was paralyzed from the waist down. A week before, a family trip to Steamboat Springs, Colorado, had highlighted the best ski season of Bill Lieser's life.

Bill's greatest support during his rehabilitation came from his biggest supporter: his wife, Mary Lee. They met in the early '60s when they both worked for the CIA. That's CIA, as in Central Intelligence Agency, not Culinary Institute of America. They were based in the Washington, DC, area for over 30 years until retirement. Family in Bucks County led them to Doylestown, Pennsylvania. Once there, they started a home-based travel business which they ran for 12 years. The business began interfering with their travel, so they "fired" themselves. A year later, Bill suffered his stroke. It was Easter weekend.

After 11 days in the hospital in North Carolina, a medical flight provided Bill with bed-to-bed service to Magee Rehab in Philadelphia. He was at Magee for seven weeks of inpatient rehab. During the first week, he celebrated his 71st birthday. Mary Lee brought a mélange of cupcakes for all. Life changes and life goes on.

A big part of the inpatient care was physical therapy—to build muscle mass for strength, as well as re-train the nerves to find other pathways to support movement. Mental attitude plays a large role, and the therapists and resident psychologist highlighted the necessity for hard work and self-motivation. Bill was undaunted. He acknowledges it is not his nature to ask, "Why me?" He looks at life's challenges as just that—a challenge.

This attitude served him well on the long road to maximizing his mobility. His inpatient stint was followed by seven months of outpatient rehabilitation, three days a week. It was exhausting work. Local friends from 26 different households logged over 8,000 miles driving Bill and Mary Lee to these therapy sessions.

Volunteer peer mentors—prior Magee patients—offered additional support and encouragement. Valuable perspective was provided by fellow patients on the fifth floor—the floor for spinal cord injuries. They were mostly young and male and had suffered spinal injuries from auto accidents, sports accidents, failed suicide attempts and gunshot wounds. Seeing 17-year-olds facing life in a wheelchair, Bill regarded himself lucky.

After many months of therapy, Bill was released to life as he would now know it. At home, he navigates with a wheelchair, walker, and forearm crutches. Real freedom arrived with his battery-powered scooter and a specially-equipped van with hand controls and ramp. There's no stopping him now. He's frequently sighted at movies, theater, jazz concerts and clubs, restaurants, and receptions. He's a fixture at the Central Bucks Family YMCA where he is chair of the board of trustees and works out three days a week. His jacket size has increased from 41 to 43. Front-page news was generated by his entry in the YMCA 5K race, his wheelchair pushed by one of their executives. He wowed the crowd when he left his wheelchair and finished the last 50 yards solo, using his walker.

His civic duties don't end at the YMCA. He is also a member of the steering committee of Friends of the Heart Institute at Doylestown Hospital, in gratitude for their fine care after he suffered a heart attack in 2007. Ironically, this occurred while he was exercising at the YMCA. He had concluded radiation treatments for prostate cancer just six days earlier.

As a board member for the County Theater, he was curious about the new digital projector now required for all cinemas if they wish to show current releases. The projector is located 20 steps above the lobby. Using techniques and strength gained in therapy—and personal determination—he climbed those 20 steps, inspected the new projector, and descended back to the lobby, tired but victorious. He doesn't set out to inspire—but he surely does.

Bill and Mary Lee are still traveling and recently returned from an annual jazz cruise in the Caribbean. Bill eagerly describes an upcoming Disney cruise with their children and grandchildren to celebrate his and Mary Lee's 50th wedding anniversary and their respective 75th birthdays. These events will also be fitting celebrations of resurrection. Life changes and life goes on.

The Bucks County Herald, April 17, 2014

The Veteran

I met Thelma Williams at a Silver Sneakers class at the local gym. Her quiet dignity and erect posture, matching workout suits and beautifully coiffed hair, caught my attention from the first day. One morning at the beginning of class, this agile, active woman made a brief announcement: "Today is my 96th birthday," she proudly declared. Jaws dropped in disbelief, even as we applauded her. After class I approached her to ask how she would celebrate. "It's Monday," she replied matter-of-factly. "I'll do the laundry."

Two months later, she broke her dress code and attended class wearing a T-shirt with "VETERAN" printed on the back in large black letters. I wanted to learn more and invited her to lunch.

Thelma was 24 years old when the United States entered World War II. "Everyone was involved in supporting the war effort," she related. "Housewives collected fat and aluminum foil, children collected rubber bands." She wanted to help too, but her weight didn't reach the minimum requirement to enlist, so she got a job at Middletown Airport (now Harrisburg) in central Pennsylvania, stocking supplies to ship to air bases around the world.

But the urge to contribute more directly refused to go away. She preferred the navy's uniforms, but the army offered a better chance at an overseas post. She went to a recruitment office and applied. I asked if she put rocks in her pockets to add weight to her slender frame and received a gently reproving look. "No," she admonished. "They accepted me as I was." And so she entered the Women's Army Corps (WACs).

Basic training was delivered at Fort Oglethorpe, Georgia—an old cavalry post with large parade grounds surrounded by barracks. A smile flirts at the corner of her eyes as she remembers all the marching they had to do on those beautiful grounds. The fitness and discipline required by the War Department still informs her *modus operandi* as she marches to the beat in our class.

After basic training, she was assigned to a motor transport training company. "I seem to have been in the right place at the right time all my life," she exclaims. After she arrived, two incumbents moved on, in quick succession, and our feisty bantam-weight recruit became a first sergeant! All she needed now was an overseas assignment.

In April 1945, the war was winding down and bases were being consolidated. Even so, she pursued overseas training and soon received orders to report to France. She set sail in August 1945 and was in the middle of the Atlantic Ocean when the news broke that Japan had surrendered. The somber military ship briefly became a party boat as standard restrictions were lifted and everyone celebrated the welcome news. At the relocation depot, she received her assignment: Bremen, Germany. Since the railroads had been bombed out, she traveled by windowless military air transport.

In Bremen, the angel on her shoulder continued its watch. The first sergeant left for a civilian post and Thelma got the position— title, stripes, and all. She remembers working hard but also having time to explore Europe via Special Services trips. In December 1945, she spent a cold week in Denmark. By April 1946, the trains were running again and she enjoyed a trip to Switzerland—each for the grand sum of 25 dollars.

By June 1946, her years of service and overseas duty had earned her enough "points" for discharge. The famous GI Bill had passed and she could return home and go to college for free. She enrolled in a business college but didn't like it. A notice that the army was recruiting a battalion of WACs to go to Japan caught her attention. She was reinstated—stripes intact—and assigned to the Office of Quartermaster General in MacArthur's Headquarters. Her WAC detachment drilled in the gardens of the Emperor's Imperial Palace.

In Tokyo, a friend introduced her to a young serviceman in the newly created US Air Force. Within three months, they were married. In November 1946, her husband was transferred back to his native Texas, so she once again applied for discharge. When they landed on US soil, she almost wasn't allowed entry—she didn't have a passport. All her previous travels had been as a WAC and it never occurred to her to provide what was required for travel as a civilian. Within a year they were ordered back to Japan—this time she brought a passport. She and her husband now had a one-year-old son. While in Japan, a daughter was born.

Eventually they returned to the States and to civilian life, but life took a sudden turn when "Tex" had a heart attack and died. He was only 63 years old. Family connections ultimately brought her back to her native Pennsylvania. She doesn't seem impressed by her longevity. "It's all in the genes," she explains. "My mother was 106 when she died!" Even as she acknowledges her good fortune and good health, a shadow passes over her features. She recalls all the crossed out names in her address book, as family and friends predecease her.

I ask for one of her most outstanding memories, and November 2, 2013, is quickly recalled. Thelma was selected to participate in "Honor Flight"—a VIP experience for veterans held in Washington, DC, complete with motorcycle escort, memorabilia packet, and visits to all the war memorials including the Women's Memorial. "It was one of the most memorable days of my life!" she enthuses. One of the gift items she received was the T-shirt with "VETERAN" emblazoned on the back.

Another highlight occurs every May, when Thelma marches with fellow WACs and other veterans in the local Memorial Day parade. That's one Monday when the laundry just has to wait.

The Bucks County Herald, November 20, 2014

Memorial Day Parade, Doylestown, Pennsylvania, 2014

The Bluebird Guy

HE GREW UP IN BROOKLYN during the 1940s, and his parents were concerned about the scourge of polio. So every summer—to avoid urban crowds—he was taken to his grandparents' farm in rural Virginia.

He enjoyed halcyon days, full of discovery and adventure. One year, as he wandered around the farm, he was drawn to a dead snag in an old apple tree. There he found a nesting site for a pair of bluebirds. With great interest he observed the parents' progress as they successfully reared four babies. He watched as both male and female built the nest and fed the young, and he marveled at their human-like dedication to their babies and each other. His discovery that summer was the beginning of a lifelong fascination. By degrees, he became interested in nature's other creatures as well, but bluebirds remain his primary focus. Decades later, Ray Hendrick is widely known as "Ray, the Bluebird Guy." He even receives mail addressed that way—and the post office knows exactly where to deliver it.

He was 10 when he made his discovery and, on returning to Brooklyn, he pored over any book about bluebirds that he could find. In those days there weren't many, but he did learn that bluebirds, unlike woodpeckers, cannot excavate their own nest cavities.

He learned they must compete for these cavities with two of nature's toughest, most invasive, birds: starlings and house sparrows. He also learned that bluebirds like a clean house, and will usually avoid a nest box that hasn't been emptied from the prior year. The seeds of a mission were planted.

While in high school he applied and was accepted at Cornell University. Soon afterward, a recruiter from the National Farm School gave a talk to his class. Ray's piqued interest led to a visit. He fell in love with the bucolic campus and was impressed with the courses and faculty. He graduated in 1959 with a BS in dairy science. Today his course of study is called animal science and the institution is known as Delaware Valley University.

During the 1960s, he was troubled by the way DDT and postwar development had diminished the bluebird population, but was encouraged by an article about a fellow enthusiast who built nest boxes to lure bluebirds back to the area. The fire of his mission rekindled. In 1964, soon after buying a home in Doylestown, Pennsylvania, he started building and posting bluebird nesting boxes around his organic garden. To his amazement, it worked. The bluebirds returned. Today he has installed over 250 boxes in and around Bucks County, Pennsylvania, helping restore habitat to his first love. Not surprisingly, bluebirds are featured on every Christmas card he sends.

Ray is officially the Doylestown Township Ornithologist. During the creation of Central Park, "Ray the Bluebird Guy" was known to the park committee. They wanted records of birds seen in the area and made him an offer he couldn't refuse: a volunteer position with Ray donating all the time, effort, and materials required. Twenty years later, it is still a volunteer effort, but he is tickled by recent remuneration: a T-shirt and baseball cap! It is obvious, however, that Ray's motivation is not financial. He loves being out-of-doors, enjoying nature, and sharing his knowledge as he leads walks and talks throughout the county.

His energy and acuity of sight and sound belie his 78 years. He can spot or hear birds before most of us even realize they are around. And he is more than a passive observer. He actively advocates for birds, lobbying to keep strips of unmown grass and brush around pond areas and allowing meadows to form in areas too hilly for sporting fields. He recognizes the park is multi-use but like humanity, birds need habitat. They love "the edges" offered by even a thin ribbon of riparian growth. Birds need cavities as well, so he advocates for dead trees and the hollows they harbor. These too are vital to bird populations.

I participate in one of his walks. His excitement is infectious as we spot dozens of red-winged blackbirds, pairs of green heron with orange feet, a brown thrasher, a mockingbird, tree swallows, red-tailed hawks, and cardinals. We learn that visiting Europeans go wild for cardinals as they don't exist in Europe—except at the Vatican.

The entire group is amazed to spot an enormous dead bird caught in tree branches. Ray raises his binoculars. What he sees dumbfounds him. "It's a common loon!" he exclaims over and over. Native to Minnesota and other northern climes, it's an unusual sight in Pennsylvania. Even if it was migrating, he is puzzled why it would fly so low. He mulls this mystery until his attention is diverted by a magnificent osprey taking flight. "It's an osprey!" he cries. Two days later, the loon is retrieved and after testing, will be on its way to the Academy of Natural Sciences in Philadelphia, Pennsylvania, for mounting and display.

His enthusiasm is sparked by many natural wonders, but his greatest joy—that day and any other—is the sight of bluebirds nesting and fledglings leaving the box. "Ray the Bluebird Guy" has never forgotten the thrill of finding that nest on his grandfather's farm.

Ray is a founder of the Bucks County Audubon Society, a longtime member of the Friends of the Peace Valley Nature Center, and has served on the Bucks County Department of Parks and Recreation board. His chief role as a naturalist has been one of restoration and his successes have made our corner of the world a more vibrant and beautiful place. He is the current chair of the Doylestown Township Environmental Advisory Council (EAC) and is proud of a recent award for the best EAC in Bucks County. In addition to bluebird boxes, he also has contributed over 40 screech owl, kestrel and wood duck boxes.

Ray wants to give people a reason to get enthusiastic about the environment. Every day, he heads out the door to serve and explore. The compensation may be nil—but the rewards are boundless.

The Bucks County Herald, May 21, 2015

Mover Not Shaker

His college major was music theory and composition—but he claims he lacked the discipline to pursue it as a career. Perhaps. But his demeanor exudes a restless spirit which ultimately beckoned him down a different path. Originally from Brooklyn, he has also lived in Georgia (too hot), and considered Maine (too cold), and Boston (too expensive), before settling in Bucks County, Pennsylvania (just right), where his entrepreneurial nature emerged in the form of a retail antique shop named Atlanta Annie's (after a real person he knew in Atlanta).

He co-owned and managed the business for 10 years, but after that time, Jules Smith was ready to leave retail. He recognized a new niche: a market need for someone knowledgeable and trustworthy to transport fine furniture, art, and other antiques. Annie Hauls was born.

I asked if he was a Woody Allen fan. "Well," he rejoined, "there's that—at least for those of us of a certain age." In reality he chose the moniker to link his former business with his new one. The new venture was a natural evolution of his reputation and expertise and fulfilled a desire to do something physically active.

Twenty-one years later, the business has three full-time employees, one part-timer (with specific expertise in shipping and storing art), and two new vans. He's proud of the company's success and acknowledges that he and his employees are like a little family. He treats them that way too, offering special holiday celebrations and even seats at the symphony, sharing his love of music.

Photo of Annie Hauls team courtesy of Steven Humphreys
Left to Right: Bryan Brems, Michael Topley, Jules Smith
(center), Steven Humphreys, Kieran Gianelli

So, when transporting fragile, valuable, rare art and artifacts, what could possibly go wrong? He laughs. "We're very careful, scientific even, about what we do, so mostly the work is without drama." But there was one instance that made him sweat. He was asked to pick up a rare 1800s weathervane that had just sold at auction. The artist had made only four, and this one had been within one family for generations.

Sotheby's sold it to a dealer who bought it for a collector willing to pay $90,000 for it. The job was to transport it to the dealer on Tuesday to be picked up by the client on Wednesday. Sotheby's pointed out a delicate repair that had been made to the tail. Jules packed it with extra care but sometimes, even with our best efforts, things still go wrong. As he drove, he heard a faint "plink," and his heart sank. He knew exactly what had happened. The dealer was livid. Jules took full responsibility.

But sometimes a bad thing can turn out to be a good thing. The next morning the dealer called. He was apologetic about his reaction. Once calmed, he found an expert welder to make a proper repair on the weathervane. When the collector arrived, he was told of the situation. He examined the repair and found no fault. He left a satisfied client. Had the tail fallen off *after* he took it home, this story might not have had as happy an ending.

Given the complexities of a "white glove" transport service, I wanted to know how he trains his employees. Basically they train on the job, as does he. Every situation is unique and every job offers a learning opportunity. But first, he wants employees to know that the dollar value of an item is only part of the value and importance to a client. Then he wants them to know the market value. He discusses what's trending in the market and what's declining, expanding their knowledge beyond specific assignments.

He trains them to question dealers about specific pieces and teaches them how to properly pick up an antique chair. He encourages them to recognize and acknowledge art in a client's environment. But most of all, he instructs them to convey confidence. Clients do not welcome trepidation from those handling prized possessions.

He often serves as a consultant for resources, market trends (folk art and American primitive are "hot" right now), and design assistance, such as where to hang a heavy mirror. People like to watch them work and Jules sees this as an opportunity to both entertain and educate. This is especially true if they are assembling and setting an antique clock. "The client needs to know how to set it when we're gone," he explains.

Annie Hauls not only transports goods, it also offers setup and assembly. "Like Ikea?" I tease. He shakes his head at my joke, but acknowledges that many people don't realize that most antique furniture can be disassembled. "A large French armoire won't fit up the stairs to a Paris apartment," he points out with a smile.

One of the team's most satisfying assignments was the transport of a large 1770s Chippendale breakfront, about nine feet high and 14 feet wide, still boasting the original wavy glass. An unusual feature was a built-in butler's desk trimmed in leather and appointed with various nooks, cubbies, and crannies. The piece had to be disassembled for transport to Asheville, North Carolina. When they arrived, a party was in progress—the breakfront's arrival and assembly was to be an event. Surrounded by partygoers, the team reassembled this unique piece, being photographed throughout the process.

When finished they all stood back and admired it. A place against a large wall had been reserved for it; it was a setting that provided the space and drama the piece required and deserved. Jules smiles just thinking about it. His greatest satisfaction is to be entrusted with something rare and special and see it find its home.

Jules' client base is approximately 60 percent auction houses, custom fabricators, interior designers and museums, and includes such recognizable names as Christie's, Sotheby's, Freeman's, the Michener Art Museum, Nakashima, and—most recently—the Metropolitan Museum of Art. With a client list like this, I'm beginning to rethink my title. Jules Smith* is a Mover AND a Shaker!

The Bucks County Herald, November 19, 2015

Sadly, Jules Smith passed away suddenly on August 20, 2016, at age 60. We will miss his eloquence, humor, and bright spirit.

Part Eight:
Life's Seasons

*"For everything there is a season
...a time to seek, and a time to lose;
a time to keep, and a time to cast away...*

ECCLESIASTES 3:1; 3:6

Peace and Love Coffee House Style

IT WAS A TYPICAL MORNING run to one of the local coffee shops. Prior to retirement, I hustled in and out as fast as possible, lingering only long enough to add cinnamon atop my takeout latte. Sometimes I still do that, but now that I'm retired, I often give myself the lovely little luxury of sitting in one of the big leather chairs and sipping my latte from a *real* cup (another indulgence) and leisurely reading the paper. On a recent morning, the place resonated with a particularly lovely vibe that commanded my attention.

In the middle of the main room, a group of about seven or eight women had cobbled several little "two-top" tables into a congenial mishmash. They gathered round, laughing as they fit everyone in, teasing some of the latecomers about whether there was enough room. Of course there was, and they barely lost a beat in their conversation as everyone indeed found a seat. They were older, energized, and clearly having fun. Across the room, two men angled into the corners of the big overstuffed couch. They leaned toward one another, their conversation also animated with overlapping dialogue punctuated with finger pokes in the air and throw-your-head-back laughter. Against the wall, a lone man focused on his computer screen, typing, stopping, typing some more. After several goes, he leaned back and nodded slightly as he hit the Enter button, apparently pleased with his communication to an unseen "other."

In the main serving area, a table was filled with foreign accents—visitors to our fair town and county. A local host was describing the area and creating word pictures of the bucolic land-scapes, diverse architecture, and stimulating museums they would experience that day. They all nodded agreeably. Nearby, two young mothers juggled strollers, toddlers, hot chocolates, small toys and snacks as expertly as a tightrope artist walks a wire. In the window, a couple rose from their advantageous spot and gave each other a hug and kiss before going their separate ways. An invisible but palpable vibration, like a chanting of "Om," resonated in me. Each vignette combined with the others to create a harmonious hum, like the music of the spheres.

This kaleidoscope of activity in some ways reminded me of the coffee houses of the '60s. The coffee houses of my youth. The experience "back in the day" was different though. Edgier. Angrier. More Anti. Those coffee houses were filled with open mic ten-sions, a general agitation, and a strange sweet-smelling odor that had nothing to do with cinnamon over nonfat foam. Ah yes. Peace and love, baby. Peace and love. The coffee houses of the '60s rever-berated with the end of innocence brought on by assassinations, an unpopular war, and the reactions of a nation in transition.

Just that fast, my thoughts shifted to those who weren't at today's coffee house as we continue to struggle with many of the same issues: those who can't possibly afford a boutique cup of cof-fee; those whose bones vibrate from artillery fire in hostile environ-ments far from home; those who are unable to easily get out and about; those who live in a neighborhood that no boutique coffee shop would consider as a location.

I am sobered as thoughts of reality seep in, and humbled as I am reminded of all my blessings for which I am deeply grateful. I am grateful in general, and specifically grateful that for a moment or a season, we may experience a time of joyful innocence. Whatever your current life season, may you be able to recognize the gifts it offers and savor many precious moments. Peace and Love, baby. Peace and Love.

The Bucks County Herald, December 15, 2011

The Winter Season

"FOR EVERYTHING THERE IS A season, and a time for every matter under heaven." These beautiful words from Ecclesiastes resonate through the centuries, a distant echo gaining force and speed as it arrives in the 21st century, with the power of a bullet train—as relevant today as for the ancients.

New Year's Day has recently come and gone, and although not exactly a "season," it represents a traditional time for reflection and resolutions—as well as an opportunity to review our "purpose under heaven."

One of my male readers refers to my column as an exercise in French existentialism. I prefer to think of it as an exercise in *discernment*—a process which may still hold anxiety and angst, but hopefully also clarity and peace. Discernment—what a concept!

During my earlier decades of life, I never even consciously considered it. In retrospect, there are many times when I must have engaged in discernment—that I would go to college, move to the Big Apple upon graduation, and befriend this person rather than that person and so on.

But my decisions were all frighteningly semi-conscious at best. Now, as I move through the early phases of retirement, discernment is continually on my mind, rolling around in my thoughts like stones in a rock polisher.

My last yoga class of the year begins with the Fifth Law of Yoga, *Om Ritam Namah: The Law of Intention and Desire.* I consider how appropriate this is on the cusp of a new year. Embedded in Om Ritam Namah are questions: Who am I? What do I want? How will I serve? Familiar, age-old questions that don't get any easier as I age. I smile slightly to myself. Where's the GPS when you really need it?

I remember vividly when the whole notion of discernment finally hit my conscious mind. I was in yet another career transition and attended a retreat through church entitled, "Thank God It's Monday." The focus of the weekend was discerning our gifts and ways they could be used in the world that blended our need to earn money with our strengths and passions, moving us from soul-deadening "jobs" to spirit-fulfilling vocations. The goal was to approach the work week with thanksgiving rather than dread. Just imagine. I finally achieved this goal, but it took decades and navigation over many bumps.

Now, in retirement, my discernments are less work-related and more life-related—less about earning money—more about fulfilling my purpose. "For everything there is a season, and a time for every matter under heaven."

I feel certain that my purpose "now" is different from my purpose "then." And if not discerned now—then when? The answers to these questions have never come easily or quickly. As I reflect back over the years, it is clear that God's hand has guided me, even if—when—I sometimes resisted.

As I write, my gaze drifts out the window. It is clear that this is the winter season—probably my least favorite time of the year. And yet, winter's important purpose seems to be to slow us down as we bundle up. It offers a time to linger in front of the fire with a good book, a good friend, or just our own thoughts. A season to ask ourselves questions.

The theologian and philosopher Meister Eckhart encourages us to do exactly what we would do if we felt most secure.

Winter encourages us to slow down enough to consider what that might be. Winter is a quiet season enabling our ability to listen to our words. How many times a day do we say "should"? How different would a day or life be if we substituted "want"? And, do our words express enough gratitude for our blessings?

Winter is a time to listen to our bodies, to become attuned to the subtle messages conveyed in our posture, our energy, our guts, and those little hairs on the backs of our necks. Bodies rarely lie, but too often the pace of our daily lives mutes their wisdom. Winter is a season and time of hibernation. Let us embrace winter's purpose as much as possible to give ourselves the gifts of stillness, quiet, and rest. "For everything there is a season, and a time for every matter under heaven."

The Bucks County Herald, January 19, 2012

'Tis the Spirit

LIKE A RISING TIDE ENCROACHING on a shoreline, the ever earlier start of the holiday buying season has been slowly inching up on us. The commercial message to buy, buy, buy has continually lapped at the edges of our consciousness. And now, in December, we are swimming in a frenzy of spending for gifts, decorations, and entertaining. While I do enjoy the festivities and gift buying, I—like so many others—wonder how we can maintain a soulful spirit in our endeavors when crass commercialism eddies around us for so many weeks and months prior. The situation reminds me of a newspaper clipping I saved from years ago:

> *"Tis the spirit in which the gift is rich*
> *As the gifts of the wise ones were—*
> *And we are not told whose gift was gold*
> *Or whose was the gift of myrrh."*
> E.V. Cooke

This little poem emphasizes not the gift but the spirit with which it is given. Spirit more than trumps the gift itself. It also emphasizes that gift giving is not a competition and we need not compare our gift to another's to determine its worth. What really defines any true gift, small or large, tangible or intangible, expensive or humble, is the sincerity and intention of the giver.

Desmond Tutu, South African social activist and retired Anglican bishop, famously said, "Do your little bit of good where you are; it's those little bits of good put together that overwhelm the world." There are so many bits of good that we can offer the world. Some are tangible but so many are not. Recently I was backing up my SUV in a crowded parking lot when a man nearby starting yelling and waving his arms. Another SUV directly behind me was backing up at the same time. We were inches away from a double rear-end collision. That unknown man did a little bit of good where he was—and saved me and the other driver time, money, upset, aggravation, and potential injury.

There are so many ways to do a little bit of good right where we are. Hold open a door, review a business you like, send an email or card, make a phone call, write a note, pay a sincere compliment, play with a child, babysit, walk a dog, shovel a neighbor's sidewalk, pay for someone else's coffee, loan a book…or even just smile.

While traveling last summer, my husband and I stopped by a small-town restaurant for breakfast. The service was slow and we were hungry, so irritability was starting to creep into our chit-chat. Finally, the frazzled waitress appeared with our brimming platters and coffee. With the crisis averted, magnanimity quickly replaced annoyance and I was able to offer a big smile of appreciation.

We ate, we paid, and as we left the café, the waitress came running out the door after us. "Uh-oh," I wondered. "Did we forget to leave a tip?" A tad breathlessly she told us she was having a difficult morning and had really needed a smile—just a smile. Getting one was a gift. She wanted to say thank you. I felt humbled and a tad embarrassed. It was a good reminder that everyone we meet is fighting a battle we know nothing about. Mother Teresa reminds us not to worry about numbers. Rather, be kind to one person at a time and start with the person nearest you.

This experience held a lot of lessons for me: lessons about the importance of little bits of good; lessons about being impatient; lessons about what might be going on for someone else; lessons about receiving a gift. There are so many ways to overwhelm the world, right where we are.

While re-reading Cooke's lilting verse, its rhythmic waves uncovered another pearl of wisdom for me—an implicit reminder that the spirit with which we receive a gift is just as important as the giving. *"We are not told...whose gift was gold or whose was the gift of myrrh."* We are not told. The recipient displayed grace and appreciation for *all* the gifts. One was not valued more than another, because the giving spirit was the same. Giving seasons are not only about giving, but also receiving.

My thoughts return to the frazzled waitress. Which of us had the greater richness of spirit? Who made the greater effort and displayed more courage? She did. Was I a gracious recipient? I hope so. But I must admit to feeling that of the little bits of good we exchanged that day, clearly hers was the gift of gold.

The Bucks County Herald, December 18, 2014

The Cruelest Month

With apologies to T.S. Eliot, I'm starting to think, even after just two weeks, that February may actually be the cruelest month. Call it cabin fever, snow and ice accumulation, fatigue, Dayquil and Nyquil overkill or whatever, I've had it. For December and January I was Miss Pollyanna. But no more, no more.

The snows of December seemed season-appropriate and very beautiful, giving a festive air as final touches were put on holiday shopping and preparations. They were light fluffy snows with enormous flakes that flaunted their individuality—a starfish here, an icy web there, little tiny babies' hands waving everywhere. All were exquisite and oh so mesmerizing.

We reveled in a squall through beautiful farmlands as we drove to my girlhood home in Buffalo for Christmas with my siblings. The giddy swirl of flakes was accompanied by the uplifting Handel's *Messiah* on the radio, creating a Currier and Ives lead-in to Christmas Eve as we wound our way in our CRV sleigh, cheerfully singing along with "The Hallelujah Chorus."

Even in January, even with one icy storm, even with leaving the house for the airport one Tuesday morning at 10:00 a.m. and not arriving home until 4:45 p.m., the morning-after beauty still astounded. "My Lord, what a morning," I would repetitively announce to no one in particular as the sun shone on a landscape where sharp edges were now all softly rounded, whose surfaces glittered like diamonds in some Disney fairyland.

I'm not a fan of snow and ice any more than most people, but the serene aesthetic after a seasonal storm can still take my breath away. Apparently many artists felt the same, given the plethora of lovely wintertime renderings by Redfield, Schofield, and Sotter, to name just a very few.

My early winter observations were a privileged indulgence. As a retiree, I rarely had to navigate in any of it. Except for the airport trek, I was not needed anywhere and so had no reason to even leave the house during or after a storm. I also didn't have to deal with any "snow day" school closings leaving me to juggle spur-of-the-moment childcare or deal with the energies of overly housebound children. To have such artsy musings about the splendor of winter is the epitome of luxury.

But now, now it is February. The snows of February have not been light and fluffy. The sun does not shine the next morning. The skies remain gray. These snows have been heavy and wet and destructive. Our beautiful border of arborvitae has been bowed and, in some cases, broken—revealing views not formerly seen and better left that way. A good-sized tree branch from a tree in our yard snapped and fell, damaging our neighbor's new fence. The snows of this February were offering no redeeming aesthetic value—merely the frozen reminder of destruction.

We are lucky. We were not among the 90 percent of residents without electricity, and none of the fallen branches landed on our cars or went through our roof or a window. Not yet anyway. We have commitments but not jobs; we have young grandchildren but not young children. Even so, I am grumpy, grouchy, and grinchy. I am heartsick about the damage to our trees, especially the taller, more established ones which have previously been impervious to storms of all sorts. I feel sorry to have added to our neighbor's woes, as she is single and has been dealing with several other home issues all on her own. I am anxious to return to my exercise and walking routines. I will be glad to see the back of February.

Regardless of whatever month is deemed the cruelest, February—thankfully—is the shortest.

The Bucks County Herald, February 20, 2014

Om Daksham Namah

I AM STRETCHED OUT ON my yoga mat in *Shavasana,* or corpse pose. As the last position in a yoga class, it is intended to be a final relaxation, allowing participants to meditate upon and absorb the day's practice. Our leader intones the spiritual law for the day, *Om Daksham Namah: the Law of Least Effort.* Om Daksham Namah means "My actions produce maximum results with minimal effort." It's the old 80/20 rule. Om Daksham Namah. I realize I am badly in need of the "Law of Least Effort" right now.

I look around my dining room. It resembles a UPS station with packages wrapped and stacked to ship to friends in New York and Arizona, a grandbaby in New Mexico, a son in New Jersey, a niece in Massachusetts and another in New York. Presents for a grandson's upcoming second birthday are stacked in another corner. Cards for family and friends experiencing the joys and challenges of life are stacked on the table awaiting a handwritten note, address, and stamp. A son is getting married, so a facial and mani-pedi are needed. A colonoscopy is scheduled.

My email and dashboard light show I have a major need for maintenance on my vehicle—the one we will drive for a 10-day road trip. A beach towel adorns our kitchen floor, soaking up the water from a refrigerator that seems to have sprung a leak. Statements from two different Visa cards, cancelled due to "potential fraud," await examination to identify all automatic payments so that we may contact the payees and change the numbers. My hair is out of control and I'm hoping to cajole my stylist into working me into her schedule before we leave town.

My husband has a grant application due on Monday and we have two of our grandchildren for the weekend. We also have four adult children joining them for a Father's Day cookout...and a two-year-old's birthday celebration. For these things I need to shop and prep and set tables.

We squeezed in a meeting with our financial planner and I'm working on estate planning, including a tour of cemetery plots and identification of specific bequests. I say I will do this before every trip—this time I'm trying to make it happen. My book editor and I have a mini-retreat scheduled before I leave, so hopefully I can work on the book over the summer.

A new grandbaby is on the horizon in New Mexico and we have much baby equipment and clothing and supplies to pack up and take with us. I'm also trying to sort out existing toddler summer clothing to redirect it to an appropriate cousin while it might still fit. Another grandson wants to "sleep with Mema," and so we squeeze in a visit.

Book club is meeting and I should just cancel, but it is such an interesting book and the discussions are always so good I hate to miss it.

So, I tell myself, this is active retirement. Or is it actually hyperactive retirement? Increasingly I'm feeling my retirement years have pushed me over the edge into ADHD.

I am attending an event and sit next to a woman I've not met before. We strike up a conversation. She tells me she has retired from a professional position. I ask what she does with her days now. "As little as possible," she replies. I am stunned. What? She was, of course, being facetious—she was at the event, after all. But upon reflection, I realized her response may have held more than a kernel of wisdom. It reminds me of that spiritual law of yoga— Om Daksham Namah: My actions produce maximum results with minimal effort. It's a concept I need to embrace.

June 2015

Solstices and the Power of Paradox

I WAS LISTENING TO A gardening report on the radio recently and it was describing the behavior of hydrangeas. On gray, rainy days they droop. But when the sun comes out, they straighten up and look alive again. I think I'm a lot like a hydrangea. The summer solstice—the longest day of our calendar year and the beginning of summer in the northern hemisphere—has just passed. The paradox, of course, is that as summer begins, our daylight gradually diminishes. It is a bittersweet time for me. I love summer and I love light.

Ten years ago, I accompanied a local choir on their tour of St. Petersburg, Russia, and Tallinn, Estonia. We traveled in late June and early July. It was an exceptional trip filled with many highlights and special memories. One of my favorite recollections is the experience of White Nights (*Beliye Nochi*) in St. Petersburg. This phenomenon is due to the city's latitude (59 degrees, 57' north)—a latitude so high that the sun, from mid-June to early July, does not descend below the horizon enough for the sky to grow dark. Night becomes indistinguishable from day. Street lights are not needed during Beliye Nochi. We could leave a restaurant at 10:00 p.m. and walk back to our hotel in daylight. We could walk at midnight on the deck of our cruise ship and see far horizons. We could awaken in the early morning and feel refreshed even after only a few hours' sleep. It was magical.

In his memoir *Memories, Dreams, Reflections*, psychoanalyst Carl Jung wrote that in order to understand his own culture, he felt it necessary to find "an outside point to stand on." In other words, he needed an opposite perspective. To that end, his travels often took him among primitive (his term not mine) peoples so that he might better understand Europeans. One trip took him to the American Southwest, "... to visit with the Indians of New Mexico." There, "...for the first time [he] had the good fortune to talk with a non-European—that is, a non-white."

A chief of the Taos Pueblos offered rare insight into his tribe's deepest beliefs and values when he pointed to the sun and said, "The sun is God." Careful questioning and listening unearthed the belief that, through rituals, they daily help [the sun] to cross the sky. "We do this not only for ourselves," declared Ochwiay Biano, "but for the whole world." Jung attributed the dignity of the Pueblo people to the cosmologically meaningful significance of their daily rituals. The Pueblo natives offered daily rituals to help the sun in its journey across the sky. It was their *raison d'etre*.

Jung's next journey took him to paradisiacal, primordial Africa. Here, the natives focused on the *moment* of the sun's daily birth, when the piercing rays of light shot forth like an arrow, as the darkness suddenly transformed into light. It was the most sacred experience of the day. It was this moment of initial light, rather than the sun itself, that became God to them. Jung reflects, "At that time I understood that within the soul from its primordial beginnings there has been a desire for light and an irrepressible urge to rise out of the primal darkness."

The sun and its light are important to us as human beings. So, of course, are the night and its darkness. The people living at the source of the Nile found the two principles of light and darkness of equal power and significance. Jung emphasized the importance of paradox to our growth. He postulated that the "tension of the opposites" pushes us toward creative transcendence, enabling new solutions to old problems. Perhaps this is why we often need the dark to "sleep on" a problem before we are able to "see the light." Jung felt paradox enabled personal growth which he called *individuation*: i.e., the constant development of one's possibilities.

In Chinese philosophy, the darkness and the light are called yin and yang. The dual symbol depicts how opposite forces are actually complementary. Together they create an interconnected and interdependent unity. In the symbol for yin, there is a dot of light. In the symbol for yang, there is a dot of darkness. In the heart of the one, is the beginning of the other.

I love summer and I love light. And yet, embedded in the beginning of one is the gradual loss of the other. The winter solstice, however, does just the opposite. At the cusp of cold dark winter, we embrace the gradual increase in the length of our days. The light grows, even in the cold heart of darkness.

The life lessons embedded in the opposites of dark and light will keep my mind busy, mulling myriad levels of meaning and understanding, even as my body relaxes into the lazy days of summer, with their ever decreasing light. Until, of course, we turn the calendar page to December 21—quite possibly my favorite day of the year.

The Bucks County Herald, July 16, 2015

"The Irrational Season"

DURING THE 1970s, MADELEINE L'ENGLE, author and former librarian at the Cathedral Church of St. John the Divine in New York City, wrote a series of essays entitled "*The Irrational Season.*" Each essay addressed a different season of the liturgical calendar. One essay on Advent and Christmas ends with a poem:

> "*This is the irrational season*
> *When love blooms bright and wild.*
> *Had Mary been filled with reason*
> *There'd have been no room for the child.*"

I have always loved this passage, but in this particular election cycle, the notion of an "irrational season" has taken a different turn in my mind. It's not one where love or reason seems to be blooming. Having withstood many presidential elections, I have at times been elated at the outcome and at times dismayed, but both the United States and I have survived. It's the democratic way. Sometimes our candidate wins, sometimes they don't. That's the way it is. All the hysteria that can be mustered won't change anything—until the next time there's an election. And yet, the finger pointing and vitriol continue to rage. Is it just me, or does this seem irrational?

But I don't think that's what L'Engle meant. Actually, I know it's not.

And what about the several states that have gathered petitions to secede from the Union, Texas foremost among them? I understand the symbolic protest inherent in their action, and grant their democratic right to that protest. But one politician has vowed to change his middle name to SECEDE (his caps, not mine) and run for office on that platform. Sam Houston, best known for his role in bringing Texas into the Union as a constituent state, was removed from his governorship for refusing to pledge an oath of allegiance to the Confederacy during the Civil War. This, in spite of his earlier effectiveness as a military leader, which ensured the independence of Texas from Mexico. One is tempted to categorize such over-the-top theatrics as irrational.

But I don't think that's what L'Engle meant. Actually, I know it's not.

This Thanksgiving, several retail employers found it necessary to start Black Friday on a national holiday—a holiday shared by all Americans regardless of faith or ethnicity. Countless dinners were disrupted coast-to-coast—not just for the employee—but for all those gathered around the table. Given the several weeks remaining for holiday shopping, carving a few hours more out of anyone's turkey feast strikes me as unnecessary—and irrational.

But I don't think that's what L'Engle meant. Actually, I know it's not.

So what did L'Engle mean by the irrational season? I believe Madeleine L'Engle's poem is a summons—a summons to me, and to each of us, to rise above the noise. A summons to open our hearts, not close them—even beyond reason. It is a summons to see that which unites us, rather than divides us—even beyond reason. She bids us to entertain mystery and miracles, not presume doom—even beyond reason. She calls us to embrace humility and recognize the limits of our control in the grand sweep of the universe.

L'Engle's "irrational season" is an invitation *to leave room for the child*: to leave room in our hearts for Potential; to leave room in our minds for Possibility; to leave room in our souls for Hope. She calls us to make space for the human spirit so that it may soar, so that it may be like a child, pure and unafraid. She entreats us, at least for a time, to surrender to that which is too monumental to comprehend. What better time to surrender than in the irrational season—when all is beyond reason?

The irrational season of Madeleine L'Engle is not a season of agitated psyches. It is not a season driven by anger or fear, greed or power. The irrational season of Madeleine L'Engle is about faith and trust. It is an extraordinary gift: a gift given and received only "When love blooms bright and wild." Whatever season you may be experiencing, I wish you the gift of the child.

*The Bucks County Herald, January 19, 2012 *

It was interesting to me to re-read this article from four years ago and realize that Ecclesiastes got it right once again when he admonished us that "there's nothing new under the sun"!

ACKNOWLEDGEMENTS

I am filled with gratitude for the support of Bridget Wingert, the editor-in-chief of the *Bucks County Herald*. She is one of the loveliest, smartest, no-nonsense professionals with whom I've had the pleasure of working. Thank you, Bridget, for giving me the opportunity to manifest my decades-old dream of being a writer, and keeping me on the straight and narrow as I did so.

To my dear husband, thank you, thank you for offering and supporting the idea for this book and for the small addition we made to our home that provided the writer's requisite "room of one's own." I also appreciate the generously given time alone that minimized distraction as I focused, often late into the night, on compiling this book.

My thanks to my family for granting permission to publish articles that often offer personal reflections. Based on the large number of responses I received when they were first published, these articles have had a special resonance with readers.

A good editor is worth her weight in gold, and although she's a slight woman, my editor Alice Lawler has added significant weight and gravitas to the planning and execution of this book. Her grace, taste and Virgo precision have added a special polish and nuance that has elevated my work to a higher level. Her encouragement and support have been significant motivators in propelling me forward when I felt ready to give up. I could not have done it without her. Any errors that may still exist are mine and mine alone.

Thanks and appreciation to my beautiful sons, who granted permission to publish essays pivoting around their lives. You continue to light up my life.

Friends, of course, must always be acknowledged for the love, laughter and support they offer for ever so many life situations. To the Luncheonettes, my yoga group, my walking buddies, my Silver Sneakers pals, and the Icon Group—especially Siri Hurst for her permission to eulogize her husband, Dr. E. Gerald Hurst; to Oliver Flint, Bucks County Choral Society, for his spirit-capturing photo of Gerry; to my special friends Sally Johnston, Joyce Molloy, and Joyce Hartman Diaz; to my sister, friend, and ever faithful cheerleader, Patti Jankowski; and to so many others—too numerous to name individually—huzzahs!

To the lovely-in-every-way Caitlin Mowrey Frederick, I offer my thanks for a candid and flattering author photo, and appreciation for all the ways she makes me look and feel good.

To all those generous souls who gave of their time and their stories for the segment entitled "Extraordinary Ordinary People," knowing you has been a gift unto itself. Allowing me to share your stories has been the icing on the cake. Heartfelt thanks to: Mary Ann Nissley, Ray Gray, Cristina Sullivan, Bill Lieser, Thelma Williams, Ray Hendrick, and Steven Humphreys on behalf of Jules Smith, now deceased.

I send special thanks to those who offered gracious praise for my book: Wendy Fulton Steginsky, a beautiful lyrical poet, now working on her third book of poems; Kathleen Zingaro Clark, writer and history lover, who has published three titles with Arcadia Publishing Company; David Campbell who gently edited my submissions for the *Bucks County Herald;* and Henry Harvey, prolific author and sculptor. In addition, I appreciate the support and assistance of writer Harry Groome, author of *The Best of Families,* who entertained my out-of-the-blue request for a networking meeting, despite never having met me. Not only have these wonderful people served as inspiration for my own publishing aspirations, they have offered sound advice and feedback.

To the wonderful people who manage collections, archives, and the rights to their own work, thank you! The following have made the chore of getting permissions a delightful adventure: Michael D. Sherbon, Associate Archivist, Pennsylvania State Archives; Sara C. Good, Collections Manager, the Mercer Museum, Bucks County Historical Society; Helen Stiefmiller, Archivist, Oklahoma City Memorial and Museum; Michelle Gallagher Roberts, Head of Registration & Collections, New Mexico Museum of Art; Victoria Addison, Addison Rowe Gallery owner, Santa Fe, New Mexico; David Coverly, cartoonist; and John Horne, Coordinator of Rights & Reproductions, National Baseball Hall of Fame Library. I also acknowledge Elizabeth Alexander, composer of "Tomorrow, God Willing," for permission to use her name, composition title and select lyrics.

For my erudite and painstaking beta readers, Sue Walsh, Joyce Molloy, and Steve Rock—thank you for adding your "fresh eyes" perspective to the final editing process. You are the polish on my apple, the icing on my cake.

It has been said you can't tell a book by its cover, but graphic designer Genevieve LaVO Cosdon has managed to do just that. I appreciate how she captured the book's themes of both literal and figurative journeys.

And finally I offer an abundance of gratitude for my readers. For some writers it may be enough simply to write. For me, it is also important to be read. Your emails, notes, letters, and verbal comments have been a gift to me—you too have kept me on the straight and narrow, as well as inspiring me to be better and do more.

Writing has been a growth experience that has helped clarify my thoughts and experiences and the words used to express them. It is a dynamic process that has taken me down paths requiring much research and the need to learn new things.

Writing has a more rebellious nature than I initially realized, and my articles often demonstrated a mind of their own as I tried to wrestle them to completion. Writing has taught me much, and has been a gift in so many ways.

A friend once reminded me of the Meister Eckhart quote, "If the only prayer you ever say in your entire life is *thank you,* it will be enough." It is a powerful prayer because it shifts our awareness to what we are grateful for, thereby expanding our lives.

Thank you—I am grateful for you—all of you. You have expanded my life. I hope in some small way I have also expanded yours.

Kay G. Rock, November 2016